WITHDRAWN

Date Due

Ordinary *Moments*
The Disabled Experience

Ordinary Moments
The Disabled Experience

Edited and with photographs by
Alan J. Brightman, Ph.D.

HUMAN POLICY PRESS
SYRACUSE

Human Policy Press
Syracuse University
P.O. Box 127
University Station
Syracuse, New York 13210

Copyright © 1985 by Human Policy Press

This book is protected by copyright. All rights, including that of translation into other languages, are reserved. No part of this book may be reproduced, stored in a retrieval system, or transmitted, in any form or by any means, electronic, mechanical, photocopying, recording, or otherwise, without the prior written permission of the publisher.

Library of Congress Cataloging in Publication Data
Main entry under title:

Ordinary moments.

   1. Physically handicapped—United States—Biography.
I. Brightman, Alan.
RD796.A2073   1983   362.4'092'2 [B]   83-10279
ISBN 0-937540-11-0

Contents

Acknowledgments .... *vii*

INTRODUCTION 1
Alan J. Brightman

Chapter 1 *IF I WERE A CAR, I'D BE A LEMON* 9
Denise Karuth

Chapter 2 *THE WAY I SEE MYSELF* 33
Don Zimmermann

Chapter 3 *BEING DEAF AND SURPRISED* 51
Nancy V. Becker

Chapter 4 *MY BODY IS NEW TO ME AGAIN* 67
Debbi Talshir

Chapter 5 *RIDING THE IRON WORM* 79
Ed Long

Chapter 6 *I WOULD BE THIS WAY FOREVER* 99
Meg Kocher

Chapter 7 *EXCEPT FOR MY LEG* 111
Stephen Spinetto

Chapter 8 *THE SOMETHING THAT HAPPENED BEFORE I WAS BORN* 127
Marsha Saxton

IMPRESSIONS 141
Alan J. Brightman

Appendix *SOME PERSONAL FAVORITES* 149

Acknowledgments

Ordinary Moments exists because two individuals thought the idea of a photo exhibition honoring the International Year of Disabled Persons made sense, and because they saw to it that what made sense would be supported with the funds to make it happen. To Geno A. Ballotti, Director of the Permanent Charity Fund of Boston, and to Richard R. Rowe, President of the F. W. Faxon Company, thanks for believing. I am deeply grateful.

To the individuals of *Ordinary Moments* who labored with love over their every word, my thanks for sticking with it, for making it fun and for continuing to teach. I hope you're pleased with what we've accomplished.

To Gail Martin, who gave enthusiastically of her time and her skills in the preparation of draft upon draft, there are, fittingly, no words to express my gratitude.

To Cynthia Bedient and Gail Sallop, whose interpreting skills are enviable, my thanks for making communication accessible.

To Joe Blatt, Bruce Baker, Linda Bourke, and Richard Brightman, thanks for being there, as always, and for caring. Your help always helps so much.

To Mary Beth Sullivan, who lived more closely than anyone with the idea and the reality of *Ordinary Moments*, thanks for your head and your equally impressive heart.

And, finally, to Dr. Michael Begab, my editor at University Park Press, thanks for the faith, then and now. Your judgments never fail to impress.

In memory of my father, Milton Brightman.
An ordinary man.
An extraordinary influence.

Ordinary *Moments*
The Disabled Experience

Introduction
Alan J. Brightman

Spatial Relations

I'm going to be rewarded in heaven. Or so I've been repeatedly told. Sometimes by teachers. Other times by parents. Mostly by fleeting observers, total strangers.

Seems like ever since I kneeled down just to play with a disabled child, somebody made it a point to predict this fate for me. Their reasoning? Most claimed I had "the patience of a saint" to be able "to work" with "the handicapped." To these observers (most of whom, in fact, never witnessed "the work"), I was capable of doing something they were not. I was special. After all, look who I chose to work with.

"I could never do what you do," is a phrase that people marked for sainthood must hear a lot.

Actually, though, I have little faith in such humbling predictions, no matter how well intentioned. My resume is just not competitive. Still, how curious it is that this knee-jerk inference of others persists. And how even more humbling it is to realize, after all, that its basis was never me, but merely *the space* I happened to be occupying when I was being observed. I was *being with* someone (or someones) about whom it's often remarked: "There but for the grace of God go I." For that, for just willingly—and, I guess, comfortably—occupying a certain space, eternal reward is presumed.

Ordinary Moments was born in that space.

Common Sense

The seeds of *Ordinary Moments* may have been planted one morning 15 years ago when I arrived for my first day as a volunteer at a large private institution for adults labeled mentally ill. I was 20 years old, curious, eager, and naive. Don Quixote was my literary hero.

I was greeted on Ward 3 by a smiling middle-aged woman loosely wrapped in a bright white robe. From one pocket hung a pen fastened with colored ribbon; from another, a ball of keys on a chain. She might have been the janitor. She was, instead, the Associate Psychologist. Following a brief but enthusiastic welcome and repeated assurances that I would find my volunteer activities "stimulating," "challenging," and other words like that, I was issued my first directive (thinly disguised as a sensible suggestion): "Why don't you read these files in order to get to know the patients?"

I was new on Ward 3, without experience and certainly without authority. Who was I to question the inverted logic, the apparent slighting of common sense? So I read.

I read about presenting problems and about family backgrounds. I read of fluctuations in test scores and in weight. I read about diagnostic hunches, treatment courses, day pass privileges, and recurrent behavioral episodes that confused and/or annoyed the staff. In files whose unnumbered pages averaged maybe an inch in thickness, I read others' descriptive phrases. Others' numbers. Others' assertions. Others' questions.

I was, on that first morning, getting to know these others quite well. I was even becoming vaguely familiar with "the patients." But, with continued reading into the late afternoon, I was still unable to develop any feeling whatsoever for the people who sat quietly in the next room, the residents of Ward 3.

I had come to this place to be with individuals. I was reading about cases. For my limited purpose that morning—to get acquainted with the residents—the files proved to be an inadequate if not misleading introduction. In real life, no one comes pre-packaged so neatly, so apparently well understood. Yet the files revealed no mystery, no complexity, no richness. They so poorly represented the people I was to get to know in the weeks and months that followed.

That the entries had been written by others is, of course, not the only—or perhaps even the primary—reason for the files' providing me with an unfulfilling introduction to the people of Ward 3. Clinical files, after all, are not intended as biographies. Nonetheless, in page after page, the obvious *presence of a mediator* proved distancing and distracting. It was through the words, interpretations and values *of someone else* (a psychologist, a medical doctor, a nurse, maybe, soon, even me) that every presentation of a person was offered. No person had been allowed to offer himself, his own words, to the account.

"Why don't you read these files in order to get to know the patients?"

Perhaps, in large institutional settings, common sense just isn't very common. There was little *getting to know* in what I'd been offered.

About Disability

When the subject is disability, we (particularly us non-disabled we's) find it hard to approach the subject casually. It stiffens us. We stiffen right back. The result: awkward, uncomfortable, self-conscious queerness. We become not quite ourselves. In the face of difference, we get different.

Perhaps stiffness is an appropriate defense against the trumpeting of heaviness that accompanies most presentations of disability. If so, it is unwarranted here; for *Ordinary Moments* is not about the *subject* of disability.

Consider for a moment the special education textbook, a form that's truly *about* disability. Just as a textbook, say, in Geography is organized by land mass, so is the textbook in Special Education organized by people mass. And just as you can go around the world in a geography text without ever soiling your socks, so can you meet all kinds of people in a special education text without ever shaking a hand, learning a nickname or sharing a laugh.

Correctly, impersonally, comprehensively, and with tidy efficiency, the special education text goes about its singular business of informing. It explains strange sounding terms and clarifies confusing concepts. It reviews the past and posits prospects for the future. Perhaps most importantly, on the night before the multiple-choice quiz on cerebral palsy or retardation (or whatever), the special education book holds your hand.

Ordinary Moments is decidedly not a textbook in the traditional sense. Its content is neither impersonal, comprehensive nor tidy. Frankly, I'm not even certain that it's all necessarily correct. Or that it needs to be. Or that it ever could be. I'm only certain that it's honest.

Ordinary Moments

Before *Ordinary Moments* was words in a book, it was photographs on a wall. The original exhibition, produced in recognition of the United Nations International Year of Disabled Persons (1981), was designed to bring people closer to images of disability that were neither didactic nor sensational. Nowhere among the 50 color prints was there a plea for charitable support. Nowhere was there a jingle or slogan or heavy message.

The photographs of *Ordinary Moments* were much like those one might take of a friend; less a display of art than an expression of familiarity and affection.

In addition to the photographs, two kinds of text were included in the exhibition. One was a collection of nine quotes, comments that had been casually tossed off by some of the individuals photographed. Originally, these were to serve as simple graphic elements in the exhibition; they would punctuate the flow of photographs in a way I hoped would be pleasant to the eye. As the exhibition traveled to various sites across the country, however, I discovered that these casual toss-offs added an important and much remembered quality to the presentation. Probably there should have been more:

1. *People should only see how they look when they're looking at me.*

2. *Ordinary is what I do. Extraordinary is what others see.*

3. *There's something nice about being special, isn't there? Isn't everyone?*

4. *Sometimes I think I'm a magnet for whispers.*

5. *It took me awhile to understand me. It'll probably take you awhile, too.*

6. *I'm not like everyone else. Neither is anybody.*

7. *Parents should hear the questions kids ask me. They'd learn something.*

8. It's hard to dance in a wheelchair. Not impossible, just hard . . . and, with the right person, wonderful.

9. I have no interest in saying, "Look at me." I have a huge interest in saying "Don't look away."

The other piece of exhibition text was titled "A Personal View" and represented my attempt to explain why I called the exhibition what I did.

A Personal View

Ordinary moments are notorious for their insignificance. Handshakes and daydreams. Whispers and wanderings. An intimacy here. An exuberance there. Light touches of silliness throughout.

Such is the unremarkable stuff of ordinary moments, pointless punctuations in any day. And such is the stuff that individuals with disabilities are presumed not to have. For what could be further from ordinary than exceptional? Or special?

Out of the ordinary is where disabilities are generally thought to reside.

"We" satisfy our days with ordinary moments. "They" shore theirs up with careful plans. "We" change our roles to suit the occasion. "They" remain the disabled everywhere. All the time. Their condition, we believe, makes our kind of ordinary moments unlikely in their lives. All their moments, we guess, are as special, as unordinary as they.

Insurmountable odds. Tiresome telethons. Unrelenting challenges. While we ease through our days, they must cope continually with theirs. In a chronic state of plight, ordinary must be a luxury. When sadness abounds, silliness makes no sense.

So goes our perception. And our language.

So continue out myths. And our misconceptions.

The people of Ordinary Moments are, in fact, as silly as anyone I know. And as serious.

Like you, each is mostly like no one else. One is quiet, reflective, surrounded by music of his own making. Another laughs often, openly, infectiously. One impresses with her savvy. Another with his simplicity.

There is, though, one commonality among the individuals of Ordinary Moments. Irrespective of their particular disability, each is handicapped in precisely the same way. Each draws the stares and sneak-peeks of the streets. Each hears the whispers, tsk's, and echoed curiosities of strangers. All are accustomed to the awkwardness of others.

None is perceived as ordinary, as just another not-so-special human being.

That's the sadness. And the significance.

That's the handicap that matters. Ordinarily.

On Whose Behalf

With the exception of infants and young children, there may be no other group of individuals on whose behalf more is spoken and from whom less is heard than the estimated 500 million people around the world termed "disabled." Of that group, the eight included in what follows represent roughly one one-hundred thousandth of one percent.

It's fair to conclude that *Ordinary Moments* will never be mistaken for an empirically sound examination of the disabled experience. But that judgment need not rest on sampling inadequacies alone. Fact is, there is absolutely nothing objective about this enterprise. *Ordinary Moments* is just eight people with something to say . . . and a ninth who benefited enormously from listening to them. If there's any pretension here, it is my own; I guessed that you might gain from listening, too.

The words in what follows were not prompted by a common set of questions, nor were they guided by what an interviewer deemed noteworthy. In each chapter there are simply stories about a life, accounts selected and developed by each individual to initiate familiarity, to begin to describe what it's like.

None of the chapters represents a category of disability; the authors here speak only for themselves. Are they, then, *typical* in some way? Can one generalize from their narratives to the experiences of others with disability? Certainly. And certainly not. But it matters little. For it is hoped that you will come away from this series of chance meetings less with an education than with an acquaintance, less with a knowing than with a feeling.

Ordinary Moments is not about the subject of disability. It is rather about eight individuals who live in a society largely ignorant of the disabled experience, a society that continues to view disability as an object of study and disabled people as poster children.

Perhaps, then, *Ordinary Moments* is, more than anything else, about you.

Two Inspirations

1. Ginny is a dwarf. Not long after her 14th birthday, she met Gibson, also a dwarf, only a few months older than she and "kinda good looking." It was a first for her, meeting someone her own age and her own size whom she knew she liked a lot.

They went to a couple of parties, not together though they spent most of their time near one another. Then, Gibson asked her to the school's first dance.

As Ginny later recalled: "That's when I first learned what my friends meant when they'd talk about how terrific slow dancing can be."

2. Laurie is blind, a little older than Ginny but no less concerned with the pressures of her peers. Not long ago, she and several friends determined to "finally see what drinking is all about. Not to get drunk. Just to try it a little." At the appointed time, they told their parents they were going to the new Travolta movie; no reason mom or dad would doubt it.

When Laurie returned home, her breath waving in front of her like a flag, her mother was still awake. "So how was it?" she asked. And Laurie launched into the prearranged critique, punctuated with anecdotes learned and rehearsed from newspaper reviews. Mom sat intentionally silent, occasionally sniffing, giving Laurie nothing to read.

"That's what's really a drag about being blind," Laurie lamented after her week-long grounding had passed. "None of my other friends got punished. It was so much easier for them to lie."

Ginny and Laurie are two young people with very obvious disabilities who have plunged into the mainstream and come up dripping with ordinariness. Ask, and they'll tell you *that's* what's important to them. Watch, and you'll see that it's these ordinary moments that fill up their lives, which, when appreciated, give a more accurate quality of understanding to the experience of disability.

That's also what *Ordinary Moments* is all about.

Chapter 1

If I Were a Car, I'd Be a Lemon

Denise Karuth

Tell Them You're a Handicapped Apartment

This morning the plumber for my building stopped by. I assured him that my barking Labrador retriever wouldn't bite by explaining that she was a seeing eye dog.

"You aren't blind are you?"

"Yes, but I used to be able to see better."

"But you're . . . you're in a wheelchair . . . You're not," he hesitated, "a cripple, too, are you?"

"I have multiple sclerosis," I answered. "Some of us just have all the luck."

"Holy Jesus! God bless you, ma'am. I'm really sorry. God bless you. If you ever have any trouble with your sink or electricity you just call this number." He placed his card on the arm of the couch. "Call any time, even at night. Just tell them you're a handicapped apartment and they'll come right out. God bless you. Jesus God!"

Sometimes the reactions are even stronger.

I would never willingly cause pain to anyone, so it makes me sad when perfect strangers walk up to me and burst into tears. My first reaction is to think that their tears are somehow my fault. As it happens, some of the people who cry have lost family members or friends to disabling illness, and in two instances, deaf senior citizens cried from a sense of empathy and community with me. In most cases, though, the tears are shed because of peoples' bleak notions of what life must be like for me, the "helpless blind cripple."

I'm not talking only about "the man in the street." The same misconceptions are held as well by students and professionals. Back when I was "just" blind, a middle-aged man passed me on campus and remarked to his companion, "Oh my God, Martha. Look at that. She's blind!"

"Yes," I replied, "but she isn't deaf!"

Then, of course, there are the rehabilitation counselors and the doctors, professionals who deal with disabled people *on a regular basis*. How much they, too, have yet to learn. For example, during my last eye exam at a leading teaching hospital in Boston, one of the top opthalmologists said (in my presence) to three of his students: "When the retinal damage is not too severe, many of these patients can lead a normal life. But in a case like this, a normal life is impossible."

This pro may have known about my eyes. He knew very little about me.

Another doctor once told me, "You can't possibly have MS. Lightning just doesn't strike twice in the same place." Would that he had been right.

I would like to be able to sit people down and say, "Look, I appreciate your concern, but my life isn't that bad. Sure, it's not quite uninterrupted bliss, but whose life is? It's a good life. I work and play and have friends and make love and mistakes and get bored now and again just like you. So put your handkerchiefs away. First impressions aside, I'm a lot more like you than you probably imagine."

Morning Thoughts

It's 6:30 a.m., and the solar alarm clock beckons through the patio doors; it refuses to be ignored. I savor a few last moments of rest and begin to plan the day ahead. It's Saturday. My weekend shower and hairwash are behind me, as are bladder irrigation and bowel care; with regard to personal care, this should be an easy day. I read over a long list of ongoing projects and responsibilities compiled over the last 2 days and select several items to work on. (With MS, memory can be affected, and mine needs all the help it can get; hence, the list.)

What's this? A Stravinsky attack! I am back at Symphony Hall where last night I heard the Dumbarton Oaks Concerto, a piece long familiar to me from my years as a music major and an orchestral musician. I must hear it again—now—and am compelled to roll over in bed to search for it in a small box of cassettes. I find it and slip it in the deck.

Having been an orchestral musician was one of the high points of my life. Orchestral playing has to be one of the most complex and beautiful group endeavors (a team sport, if you will) yet devised by humanity. Football pales to insignificance in comparison.

As a 17 year old who had been ardently playing double bass for only 2 years, Chamber Orchestra helped me discover the exhilaration of overcoming overwhelming inexperience, the joy of sharing in the creation of something unsurpassingly wonderful, and of intimate involvement with a plane of music that I would have thought far beyond my understanding.

My intense involvement with music was like an express train to enlightenment: Regardless of what happens at the end of the line, one is always grateful for the ticket. People often wonder that I am not bitter about having to give up my orchestral playing. Sometimes I miss it so much that I cry. Mostly, though, I am grateful for having had the opportunity and for having learned, importantly, from it. So I cannot complain. My life now presents me with many of the same challenges and opportunities as did Stravinsky's music. The stakes, of course, are higher, but the price of defeat is more than I am willing to pay.

The joy of living with meaning and with purpose is worth considerable effort. In the long run, I do not have a great deal of control over what is happening to me physically. But if I let my physical disability paralyze my spirit, my life would become a well of self-pity, anger, and despair. I cannot allow that to happen.

The Normal Aspects

What's my life been like? I was born 2 months prematurely in November 1954, the middle child of three. My family lived in the Adirondak Mountains and in Buffalo, New York. I attended public schools in Cheektowaga and Amherst, both neighbors to Buffalo. In 1972 I won a New York State Regents' Scholarship that paid my tuition to the State University of New York at Buffalo. In 1976 I graduated magna cum laude with a degree in music. That September, my brother Ed, our closest friend Fred, and I moved to Boston where I attended graduate school and received a master's degree in rehabilitation counseling.

I began my work in the disabled community with Vision Foundation, a non-profit consumer organization that provides information and assistance to the newly blind, the visually impaired, and people with progressive eye disease. I answered phones, wrote and typed letters, made a telephone information tape, and facilitated self-help groups. Then, for 3 years, I was a counselor and advocate at the Boston Self Help Center. (I continue to do advocacy with numerous state and local organizations of and for disabled persons.) In addition, since 1978, I have worked extensively as a member of the Special Needs Advisory Board of the Museum of Fine Arts, Boston, concentrating on solving problems of access for disabled visitors.

I am very active in First Church in Cambridge, Congregational, where I am Vice Chairperson of the Board of Deacons and member of the Executive Council and the choir. I have also served on the Music and Other Arts Committee and directed the childrens' music program.

My faith education stressed the importance of serving others and working for justice and peace. I am a member of the local chapters of the American Friends' Service Committee, Mobilization for Survival, Amnesty International, and IMPACT, a national ecumenical political action network. I have also lobbied at both state and national levels concerning U.S. involvement in Latin America, U.S. food policy, nuclear disarmament, civil rights for the disabled, and human services legislation and cutbacks. I have supported the Infant Formula Action Coalition, INFACT, which fights the unethical promotion of infant formula in Third World countries and helped organize a Legal Defense Fund for a friend who was unjustly arrested at the Seabrook nuclear power plant site in New Hampshire (all charges against him were later dropped). I have written a review of an accessible art exhibit for the Cambridge womens' magazine *Sojourner*, and have had requests to do further writing. I also have been involved with two area food co-ops.

For fun, I run Irene, my black Labrador retriever, around Jamaica Pond every week in good weather. I entertain and visit friends, play some piano and recorder, and take walks in my motorized wheelchair either with friends or on my own.

So much for the many "normal" aspects of my life. As I focus on my experience as a disabled individual, I hope that you, the reader, will not lose sight of the similarity of the life we share.

Cousin Carol's Pregnant?

Being legally blind, with a small amount of residual vision, is like living in a bizarre fun house where what you see is not necessarily what you get. First off, I can see things up close far better than things any distance away. I can see my fingers, for example, if I hold them 2 inches from my face, but I cannot see my toes (although, when the lighting is right, I can see a blur where my foot is). If the contrast is right, I can make out Irene's dark shape; but, then, I have also mistaken a low stool or my black skirt or my black coat lying on the bed for Irene, even in the best light.

As my sight deteriorated, I found myself asking questions of store mannequins, I mistook full-length mirrors for doorways, and I tried to find the "Push for Walk" button on trees.

Many people think that either you can see or you can't. How difficult it is to write about vision, since no common vocabulary exists that adequately explains the variability of sight.

Being blind with residual vision means that you "see" your relatives and friends on the Boston trolleys and busses . . . even though those relatives never left Buffalo. It means looking both ways before crossing the street and then walking out into the side of a schoolbus. It means entering an unfamiliar room and being visually bombarded by confusing patterns of light and dark. It means getting so accustomed to familiar places that your friends accuse you of being able to see, or worse, they forget to warn you about newly placed obstacles.

Being blind means getting so thoroughly lost that sometimes you have no idea where you are, much less how to get where you're going. It means having people come up to you in the street, say "Hi!" and disappear, before you can figure out who they were. (*Always* identify yourself to your blind friends, especially if your meeting occurs in a place where they're not used to seeing you.)

Being blind means not knowing that Aunt Trudy has lost weight, or that cousin Carol is 8 months pregnant (until you embrace them). It means brushing up against wet paint, waltzing down the street with silver-streaked coat and hair, and wondering why people are taking notice of you. It means being the only person in the theater who does not dive under a chair when Audrey Hepburn's ankle is grabbed by her assailant in "Wait Until Dark." It means being utterly confused by cars making right and left turns on red. It means spending too much time looking for housekeys, dark glasses, the checkbook, or the vegetable steamer. And it means knowing how to take notes into exams by a method so wonderfully clever that I will not reveal it here.

In my case being blind is compounded by poor memory, difficulty with sense of touch, and the fact that I rely on others to do so much for me that things are often put away without my knowing where to find them again.

In short, being blind means having to become adept at assembling an image of reality from a jumble of jigsaw puzzle pieces—and doing so in the shortest possible time.

Ghosts

One winter evening, I had an orchestra rehearsal until 5:30 and a bus to catch for the dress rehearsal of "La Bohème" at 6:15. I left Baird Hall, the music building, to run across Main Street and grab a quick supper. When I left the restaurant it was dark and I slipped on some sheet ice. I heard nearby footsteps and could feel people stare. "Will the blind lady be able to get up?"

Never before had I been able to hear people without being able to see them. From the sound of their footsteps I knew they were only a few feet in front of me, but I looked for them in vain. No one offered assistance as I tried to get up, and I was too shocked to ask for help. When I regained my balance, the footsteps retreated into the night. I felt as if I'd seen ghosts.

With little time left, I headed back to Baird Hall in a rush. But I couldn't find it! Its dark plate glass windows had dissolved into the night, and its interior lights now merged with those of street lamps and other buildings. Surrounded as it was by a five-hundred car parking lot, it was even harder to locate. For me it had ceased to exist.

I raced through the lot knowing that the bus was scheduled to leave in a matter of minutes, but I couldn't find it. Finally, I got hold of myself and developed a plan: if I were to cross Main Street and locate the corner gas station, I could then cross the street again and find the hall by walking straight ahead.

With little difficulty, the plan succeeded. I had found the hall. I also found that my string bass had been locked in the rehearsal hall, and there was no custodian in the building. I burst into tears.

At that moment, a custodian returned from his supper break and, with his quick assistance, my instrument and I made it onto the bus.

The entire episode, from leaving the restaurant to boarding the bus, had lasted all of 20 minutes. In that time, I had seen ghosts and lost a building. It was 20 minutes of eerie confusion that I don't ever want to re-live.

Not a Textbook Case

MS. It stands for multiple sclerosis, a chronic, disabling, neurologic disease. In my book it also stands for the Marquis de Sade, who, if given the chance to invent a disease, would have been hard pressed to come up with anything more diabolical.

No one knows what causes MS or how to cure it. There isn't even a fool-proof diagnostic test to see if you've got it. Many MS'ers are told that their symptoms are caused by depression, anxiety, hysteria, and even conversion reaction. It's not uncommon for as many as 8 years to elapse before the diagnosis is confirmed.

MS presents with dozens of different symptoms and affects each individual who has it quite differently. Textbook cases of MS are found only in textbooks.

One of the most disabling aspects of the disease is fatigue. There are 168 hours in a week. In a good week I can spend about 15 hours away from home in a wheelchair doing things like working, socializing, attending meetings and church, and the like. About 85% of my time is spent in bed in a mixture of work, resting up, and planning ahead. Being able to condense much of life into 15 hours a week and developing strategies for a constructive invalidism should earn me an honorary degree as a management consultant.

Sticking to the Chair

In July 1979, I had a nerve block procedure done to relieve pain; the procedure caused nerve damage to my left leg that made it impossible for me to bear weight on it. Since my back, arms, and legs were too weak to use crutches or a walker for more than a few steps, I began to use a wheelchair full-time.

As the months passed and I began to realize that my new disability might be more than temporary, I felt frustrated, angry, and trapped. These reactions were intensified by my living in an area without affordable, accessible transportation (services costing upwards of $25.00 per ride might as well not have existed), in an apartment with stairs, and in a wheelchair I could not push for any distance by myself. In addition, the apartment was difficult to negotiate because of high thresholds and narrow doorways.

My initial emotions, though, were balanced by a real freedom from pain and uncertainty. The *Event*—changing from walking to riding—had happened and was over. So I carried on.

There were clients to keep in touch with, bills to pay, friends to see, letters to write, advocacy and church work to do. When I finally moved into an accessible apartment and acquired my two electric wheelchairs (the second because my first was unsuitable for outdoor use), the sense of freedom came rushing in like a wave. The second day I had my outdoor chair, I took it and Irene on an 8 mile walk, four times longer than any walk I'd been able to take in 5 years! The wheelchair had liberated me from the limits of my walking, and from a fair amount of the pain that walking and standing had intensified.

There are times now when I almost take for granted my ability to glide down streets for distances that were formerly unthinkable. I pass places where I spent hours waiting for buses to go distances I can now wheelchair in minutes. I remember how much it hurt to stand and wait for trains and buses, how I sat down on curbs and on floors of trolleys, banks, and supermarkets in an attempt to lessen the overwhelming pain and fatigue. I remember the times I cried walking down the street, doing dishes, or waiting for transit.

Walking is certainly convenient, and it was great to do while I could, but I think that people like me are sometimes enslaved by it in a society (including the medical profession) that insists on maintaining one's ability to walk at all costs, even when walking severely limits an individual's ability to function optimally.

This is not to say that being in a wheelchair is a barrier-free piece of cake. But individuals should be free to choose what works best for them.

I would love to walk again. But if walking means encountering the same degree of pain, fatigue, and limitation that I experienced earlier, I'll stick to the wheelchair, thank you.

The Littlest Dropout

School. God, I don't even want to think about school. Kindergarten was so bad I dropped out—held onto a kitchen chair and refused to go. Grades 1 through 9 weren't much better. Once I awoke trembling from a nightmare in which I was forced to return to junior high school for 2 years because I didn't complete gym.

Kids would take advantage of my slowed reactions. Teachers wouldn't let me sit where I stood a chance of making out what was on the board. I was the kid you could beat up with impunity, provided you moved quickly enough.

Grades 10 to 12 were a little less hellish. The rotten side of kids generally improves with age, and my increasing musical prowess eased the experience considerably. So did the fact that I was allowed extra time to take large-type final exams in the 11th grade.

My positive church experiences and a handful of caring public school teachers were the only reasons I didn't go completely insane.

I felt so sorry for the first generation of kids to be mainstreamed.

Inaccessible Access

The biggest environmental barriers faced by individuals who use wheelchairs are, of course, architectural. This is further complicated by the fact that, by my estimate, as much as 60% of "accessible" architecture is flawed, with about 20% posing insurmountable difficulties. Two of my favorite inaccessible accessible buildings are the Looney Tower classroom building at Boston State College where I attended graduate school and the Academy Hill Road branch of the Boston Public Library in Brighton, near my home.

The Looney Tower is an 11-story structure with imposing black plate glass windows. Since the building's first floor, called upper level, is several steps higher than street level, it was decided that a ramp would be built to the basement, called first floor. For starters, the ramp is steeper than code and extends for over 50 feet with no level resting places; this makes it extremely difficult for an individual in a manual wheelchair to climb. At the bottom of the ramp one discovers that there are no handles on any of the several doors, which means that they can only be opened from the inside of the building! Since there is no doorbell (and no reason whatsoever for anyone to visit this corner of the basement, anyway), the absence of handles makes it impossible to enter the building unless you climb back up the ramp, flag a passing stranger, and convince him or her to go into the building and let you in. The icing on the cake is that the ramp begins with 6-inch step where the new building sidewalk and the old public sidewalk meet!

Efforts to modify this situation, to convert the inaccessible accessibility, have been characterized by typical bureaucratic sensibility and wit. For example, a handle was subsequently attached to one of the doors so that it can now be opened by someone in a wheelchair—if that someone has 25 pounds of arm pressure to spare. A short "ramplet" has also been built at a point where the two sidewalks are only 2 inches apart. This "ramplet," however, is at least 60 feet away from the ramp, and unless you really have your wits about you, it's likely that you will get to the top of the ramp and roll right off the 6-inch drop. What a thrill! I was fortunate that my electric wheelchair was heavy enough that it didn't tip over. Lighter chairs would have.

The most striking architectural feature of the Academy Hill Road Library is the steep ramps that dissect its two levels. I am told that they were added to the building to meet access standards after the building was completed in the mid-70s. There is also a ground level entrance with a nice wide door in the rear of the building. "So what's the problem?" you ask. This relatively accessible building is surrounded by a curb that's 8 inches high!

When I had first called the library to inquire about access, the librarian assured me that the rear entrance was accessible. When I got there and discovered the curb, a friend who was with me went in and protested. "Well," said the librarian, "that's our most accessible entrance."

After four volunteers lifted me and my 180-pound wheelchair over the curb, I told them that "access is like pregnancy. Either you are or you aren't."

The Simple Life

It's 4:15 on a Saturday afternoon. Fred is playing guitar, Irene is taking a drink, and I'm sitting in bed. A friend in the building is having a dinner party later, and I need to think about it. Also, I need to plan for tomorrow.

Do I want bowel care today, or will it make me feel punk at the party? If I do, I'd better take a pyridium to keep my bladder and urethra from spasming. Did the clothes I want to wear make it into the wash?

Whose turn is it to ask for a ride to church? (My dislike of asking people for rides to church is outmatched only by my love of choir, which rehearses earlier than the local wheelchair transit service can get me there.) Some would think that dependency and illness simplify life in that one is no longer faced with the burdens of work and self-reliance. On the contrary, a severely disabled person generally has more details to keep track of and a harder time doing it.

An able-bodied person does not have to:

◇ *know exactly where everything is in the house (from Elmer's Glue and electrical tape to hair barrettes and catheter clamps) because the able-bodied person can easily get up and search for things. A disabled person who spends a great deal of time in bed has to be able to tell others where things can be found.*

◇ *set aside substantial amounts of time or plan in advance for things like bowel movements and catheter irrigation.*

◇ *plan activities 5 business days in advance to meet the requirements of the wheelchair transit system.*

◇ *make sure that a list of approximately 20 medical and surgical supplies are in stock and close at hand, along with whatever prescription drugs are required.*

◇ *keep a particularly close watch on the budget so he or she can afford to pay attendants even when the reimbursement checks from Medicaid are 3 to 4 months behind.*

◇ *budget time so that not more than 5 hours a day are spent out of bed.*

◇ *hassle with things like wheelchair acquisition, maintenance, and repair or bills that providers did not submit to Medicaid.*

In general, the less you are able to do for yourself, the more health problems you have that require specialized care. Also, as it gets harder to remember things, the more things there are to be remembered, planned, and kept track of.

The more disabled you are, the more of a magician you have to be simply to lead a normal life.

We Have Lift-Off

As my Personal Care Attendants say: "Getting you ready to go out is like preparing to launch the Space Shuttle." And I am not *that* disabled!

If I Were a Car, I'd Be a Lemon

I have a fair amount of use of my hands and I do not depend on a respirator or any specialized equipment.

Everything I do requires so much preparation and effort. To write I have to have my writing board, a wooden frame with 19 elastic bands stretched across it, the foam rubber sleeve that I slip over my pen, and the bamboo-wicker lap tray my sister gave me for Christmas. Before I raise the head of the bed to begin writing, I have to make sure I have everything I want or need from my bedside table since, when the bed is raised, the table is out of reach. Then I have to position myself for maximum endurance with minimum effort.

The problem is that *preparing* to do things like writing and going out is tiring in itself. In the Boston Marathon many runners "hit the wall" at a place called Heartbreak Hill. I sometimes hit the wall before the starting gun is fired.

After being blind for a time, I began to feel that I had won the struggle to overcome my disability in that I had largely found solutions to the technical problems that blindness presented. I had arrived at a point where I could accomplish, fairly independently, tasks such as working, cooking, traveling, doing laundry, shopping, and cleaning. My limitations, I believed, though real and sometimes painful, were not seriously handicapping.

Now I am less content with my situation. While it is accurate to say that I am quite active and independent for a person with my level of disability, I feel greatly constrained from enjoying the life I would like to live. When virtually everything you do is an effort, and when all efforts are tiring, the odds are stacked against you.

Usually I can pace myself fairly well, but there have been times when the preparations involved in going out proved so exhausting that, finally dressed and ready, I wound up staying home. More often, I get to where I'm going only to space out when I get there. This is especially true in the evening. Since I am usually in bed for the night by 5:00 p.m., it is easy to see why evening meetings are particularly deadly. While I still manage to contribute, the quality of my contribution decreases as the evening progresses; eventually I find myself quite alienated from what is actually happening. Too tired to follow conversations closely, I find myself listening to the different speakers and thinking: These people still have energy. They could go on for hours if they had to. I'll bet they got up this morning, worked all day, drove to this meeting, and took their abilities for granted. And tomorrow they'll be able to get up and start all over again. I'll bet none of them has ever slept 16 hours after working 8, or thought twice about the effort it takes to wind the alarm clock, or emptied a leg bag (or "urinary appliance" as the manufacturer calls it) over the drain in a laundry room because the bathroom door, 25 feet away, is only 24 inches wide.

Others may be surprised to know I think these things because I function so well in "normal" society. And that's the catch: because I function so well, I have led people to expect me to function well. How can I begin to let them know just how difficult things are without shocking them or causing them to overreact? And when the time comes to retire, how do I retire gracefully?

The worst part of all this is that I continue to expect a great deal of myself; I do not have a clear sense for reasonable self-expectations. How hard should I try? When is giving up not copping out?

I have learned the hard way (over and over again) that you can lead your friends, colleagues, and even yourself into believing that you are stronger than you are. But you cannot fool MS.

Don't Talk of Doctors

Being hospitalized for tests is what I imagine it must be like to be incarcerated and tortured; either your body finally confesses what's wrong with it, or your captors give up and release you.

My last hospitalization was a nightmare of minor aggravations and major trials. First off, my roommate chain-smoked and watched 17 hours of television a day. Also, I had to give my complete medical history to at least five different doctors in 24 hours (even though I was in episode and just wanted to sleep); was shocked with about 300 volts of electricity 480 times in 4 minutes during an EMG (a test for nerve and muscle damage which measures your body's reaction to electric shock and needle insertion); was hit on both sides of my head about 40 times to get the dye out during a myelogram (and got a spinal headache during the test); and had an extraordinarily painful cystometrogram, which my urologist later admitted may have contributed to my bladder becoming totally flaccid and atonic.

The most difficult treatment I had to endure, though, came when my bladder gave up the ghost and I could no longer urinate. I had noticed that voiding was becoming increasingly difficult and asked to see a urologist on a Wednesday night. I awoke on Thursday to discover that I could not void at all. I was allowed to distend for 15 hours and to build up a volume of 1600 cc's before the doctors, who insisted on catheterizing me only three times a day, would give the order to catheterize me. This meant my going 12 hours overnight and 6 hours during the day between catheterizations, even though each catheterization yielded at least 1200 cc's. I spent a lot of time in unnecessary excruciating pain from being so badly distended.

When I begged to be catheterized every 4 hours to counter the risk of infection and further bladder damage, my neurologist held his ground for 6 hours saying, "I could make you wait 8 (to which I replied "And I could leave here"). I suffered 5 long days of this torture before my neurologist, who was certain that my difficulty was temporary and due to long hospitalization, finally kept his daily promise and arranged for a urologist to see me. It probably helped that on that fifth night I dissolved into tears and told the nurses that I would have received better treatment if I had gone to the emergency room (and I had half a mind to do just that). I added that while I realized that hospitalization means giving up substantial control over one's life, even a prisoner can piss in the corner of his cell if he has to. Why had this most basic right been taken away from me?

Just before the urologist's visit, I was given a Foley catheter and antibiotics to treat an infection caused by the infrequent catheterization. My neurologist told me that the Foley would be out "by that night," and I would be voiding again on my own. The urologist, one of only a handful of open, honest, and non-condescending physicians I have encountered, told me, "Your neurologist is completely on the wrong track. He had me convinced that the cystometrogram results must be wrong, but after talking with you, they make perfect sense. Either your nerves are dead or your muscles are dead, but something's dead, and you're not going to be able to void on your own again." I have had a Foley catheter to this day.

The hottest place in my personal vision of hell is reserved for "professional" people who turn their inability to deal with my disability against me. It's reserved for the Special Education Department chairperson who snapped, "What are you doing in this program if you can't see?" and for the neurologist who complained, "It's clear that you have an incurable neurologic disease. Why do you care what it is?"

When I was young and naive, reactions like these were shocking and painful. Now I realize there is no excuse for such behavior, especially from professionals (presumably) trained to help.

How would you feel if the auto repairman had the same degree of control over your car that a doctor has over your body? If you had to convince him that you need a new transmission in the same way you have to convince a doctor that you need a certain type of wheelchair? If you needed a prescription to buy antifreeze or oil in the same way you need prescriptions to buy urinary supplies that everyone acknowledges you need? If the repairman was a fraction as pompous and condescending as many doctors manage to be?

My unpleasant experiences with doctors and hospitalization are by no means unique. Once, when I was talking with a group of disabled people about the social forces that help and hinder us, an able-bodied person innocently asked; "What about doctors?"

There was a momentary silence followed by a common response that sounded with the intensity of a rifle shot: "Don't ever talk to disabled people about doctors!"

Front-Line Friends

PCAs (personal care attendants) are my front-line defense against the obstacles imposed by severe disability. PCAs are individuals who I hire with Medicaid funds to assist me with all the activities of life that I find difficult or impossible. PCAs differ from homemakers in that they assist their employers with personal and nursing type care—bathing, catheter and bowel care, physical therapy, dressing, and positioning—in addition to housework and laundry. PCAs also shop, run errands, and, most importantly, cook for their employers. It is not an overstatement to say that I could not stay in my apartment without attendant care. Not long ago I would have lived with my family or in a nursing home; PCAs now enable me to live independently.

As much as I love my family, I would not want to burden them with the responsibility for my care. My parents looked after me for 20 years. My brother and sister have a right to their own lives. I am entitled to mine.

In the morning, Fred makes my breakfast, washes the dishes; gives me a bed bath, my toothbrush, and my medications; assists with bowel care, physical therapy, and catheter care; feeds and walks Irene; and generally sets me up for the day. If I am going out, he dresses and transfers me and assembles my belongings.

In the afternoon, Michael gives me a shower or bed bath, prepares supper, feeds and walks Irene, assists with physical therapy and catheter care, and either leaves me in bed for the night or dresses me and gets me ready to go out.

Before I go to sleep, Fred empties my bed bag (a large-volume urinary drainage bag that attaches to the bed), walks Irene, gives me my toothbrush and medication, sets me up for the night, and turns the lights off.

Fred, Michael, and Michael's brother Jody all share the responsibility of housework, shopping, laundry, and errands. Fred, who lives with me, also helps with odds and ends during the day and with emergencies or special circumstances at night (such as assisting with turning, letting Irene out, and handling catheter problems).

I am most fortunate in that all of my PCAs to date have also been friends. This good fortune is the result of my long association with the severely disabled community in the Boston area. Since Fred and Michael were caught in the employment glut of liberal arts degree holders, and since they both had previous experience working in health care and social service fields, I encouraged them to become PCAs. Consequently, when I became eligible for attendant services several years later, I was surrounded by well-trained, experienced PCA friends.

One example of how well these relationships have worked out occurred when I returned from the hospital in September 1981 to a radically different way of life. I couldn't transfer independently, and my sitting tolerance was about an hour per day. I had arranged for a hospital bed in the living room, a high-backed, reclining manual wheelchair, and full-time, live-in PCA help.

After my grueling ordeal in the hospital, I'd forgotten just how wonderful home can be. It was Friday and many of my friends came to visit. The weekend turned into a 3-day celebration. Fred, Michael, and Fred's brother Karl are all trained PCAs, and at least one of them was around at all times. They were more used to the personal care routine than I was, and they made sure that things (like emptying the bed bag) got done. They taught me many of the ins and outs of being severely disabled. And they did it all in a context of high times, good humor, love, and acceptance.

Many of their suggestions could come under the heading of "The Practical Side of Dealing with Catheterization" or "An Ounce of Piss is Worth a Pound of Prevention" and included aphorisms like: keep a basin under your night drainage bag, change bags over a floor and not a rug if you have a choice (especially if you are trying to do it independently), and keep a good supply of large and small size Chux (disposable underpads) handy. There were also some good laughs over the fact that my Urocare leg bag looks like a condom for the Jolly Green Giant.

After a month of having no control over my life, these friends showed me what I would have to do to take charge of myself again. After a month of sterile formality, they re-introduced me to joy, love, intimacy, and caring. It couldn't have been a better homecoming!

A friend once told me that among the reasons he enjoys being a PCA is this: It's the closest he'll probably ever come to meeting aliens. He may well be right. Many aspects of the day-to-day lives of severely disabled people are structured quite differently from those of our able-bodied peers. If you are disabled and want to lead a "normal" life, you have to have your act together.

To see what I mean, imagine yourself with a disability. Better yet, imagine yourself with a series of different disabilities and then try to see how any one of them would alter your daily routine. How might you brush your teeth, for example, if you had only one hand? How would you cross the street safely if you couldn't see the cars or the signal? How would you negotiate your workplace if you were in a wheelchair? How would you travel around if you were required to give up your driver's license because you had epilepsy? The list, believe me, goes on.

A disability becomes a handicap only when solutions can't be found to the problems that disability presents. In my mind, people who have managed to solve such problems often develop a clarity of vision and wisdom, if you will, that few can match (another aspect, perhaps, of our "alien" nature).

It can hardly be coincidence that one of our most effective modern presidents—Franklin D. Roosevelt—was disabled. As he is once reported to have said, "After you've spent 2 years in bed trying to move your big toe, you can do anything." How sad it is that in the minds of many people disability remains inexorably linked to incompetence (and that Roosevelt's use of a wheelchair, as a result, had to be kept under wraps).

This is not to say that disabled people who cope well with their disabilities are superhuman. It's just that, in my opinion, the process of learning to live with a disability presents an opportunity to develop competencies in judgment, problem solving, and compassion that few of life's other experiences can equal.

Remembering to Remember

I never realized how essential memory is to daily life until I began to lose mine. For example, you have to be able to remember what day it is—for the entire day. And when you cook, you have to remember that something is on the stove.

Sometimes you can know something and not remember it. I basically know, for example, what I have to do to get up and go out, but I often forget to allow enough time for particulars such as assembling wheelchair accessories or feeding Irene. When this forgetting began to happen too regularly, I finally compiled a list of the activities I needed to accomplish before heading out. Even after completing it, other tasks would come to mind and would be added. Now, often, I review my list the night before so that I can get things done in advance.

Here's my current list:

◇ *Take medicine*

◇ *Wash*

◇ *Eat breakfast*

◇ *Do bowel care, irrigation*

◇ *Assemble clothes, leg bag, hemostat, diaper, shoes*

◇ *Change into leg bag*

◇ *Diaper*

◇ *Dress*

◇ *Comb hair*

- ◇ Brush teeth
- ◇ Put cushion and coat in wheelchair
- ◇ Feed and run Irene
- ◇ Assemble belongings
- ◇ Assemble wheelchair parts and accessories
- ◇ Transfer
- ◇ Put on coat
- ◇ Leash and harness Irene

I also maintain a list of the belongings that I generally take with me on outings:

- ◇ RIDE tickets (for the accessible transit service)
- ◇ Dog dish and food
- ◇ Irrigation syringe and solution (if necessary)
- ◇ Wallet, keys, and IDs
- ◇ Checkbook
- ◇ Leash and harness
- ◇ Lap and transfer boards
- ◇ Medication (this item has its own sub-list)
- ◇ Dark glasses, other glasses
- ◇ Sun visor
- ◇ Pillow, wheelchair cushion, footrests
- ◇ Water bottle (filled)
- ◇ Urinal
- ◇ Writing board and papers
- ◇ Lap belt
- ◇ Chux, diaper, alcohol wipes

These two lists have simplified my life tremendously and have prevented many anxious moments trying to remember what I should be doing next, or what I might be forgetting.

But I have more than these. What follows is a list of my lists:

- ◇ Long-term projects and obligations (reviewed daily)
- ◇ Daily tasks, projects, and obligations

- ◇ *Spring cleaning tasks: a) that I can do myself; and b) that others will have to do*
- ◇ *Items to be taken on overnight outings and trips*
- ◇ *Items to be included in this chapter*
- ◇ *Personal care schedule*
- ◇ *Phone numbers*
- ◇ *Books on loan from the Library of Congress' National Library Service for the Blind and Physically Handicapped and from Recordings for the Blind, Inc.*
- ◇ *Two lists of physical therapy exercises*
- ◇ *Names and phone numbers of friends and former clients*
- ◇ *Names and addresses of out-of-town friends and family*
- ◇ *Calendar*
- ◇ *Medical and surgical supplies that must be stocked*
- ◇ *Fears and questions I have concerning life with a progressive disease*

Some of my lists are on large sheets of braille paper, others are in a loose-leaf binder. All are on cassette tape.

Given my necessary reliance on the above lists, you can perhaps imagine how difficult it is for me to read and be able to recall what I've read; to think through any kind of problem; to follow long, involved discussions, lectures, or meetings; to speak extemporaneously; sing in a choir or write. Formerly, I was on a par with my peers when it came to these activities; now I have to run just to keep up. Fortunately, I run well enough so that my difficulty rarely becomes obvious.

But I can tell that this state of affairs will not last much longer. And I find it extraordinarily difficult to be facing what amounts to senility: My train of thought makes sudden stops and radical changes of itinerary. It derails regularly.

Many mornings, it takes a fair amount of effort just to remember what day it is. I repeat: "Today is . . . Today is . . ." so that I will not forget. And I continue this process throughout the day (unless I've written it down on my list).

Bob, the choir director, says to sing in unison. I hear him, but it takes me five bars to catch on.

I take my medication, and 5 minutes later I can't recall that I've taken it.

I hang up the phone and immediately forget who I was speaking with.

I review the names of friends and family members before calling them.

I repeat questions minutes after they've been answered, and then I ask them all over again.

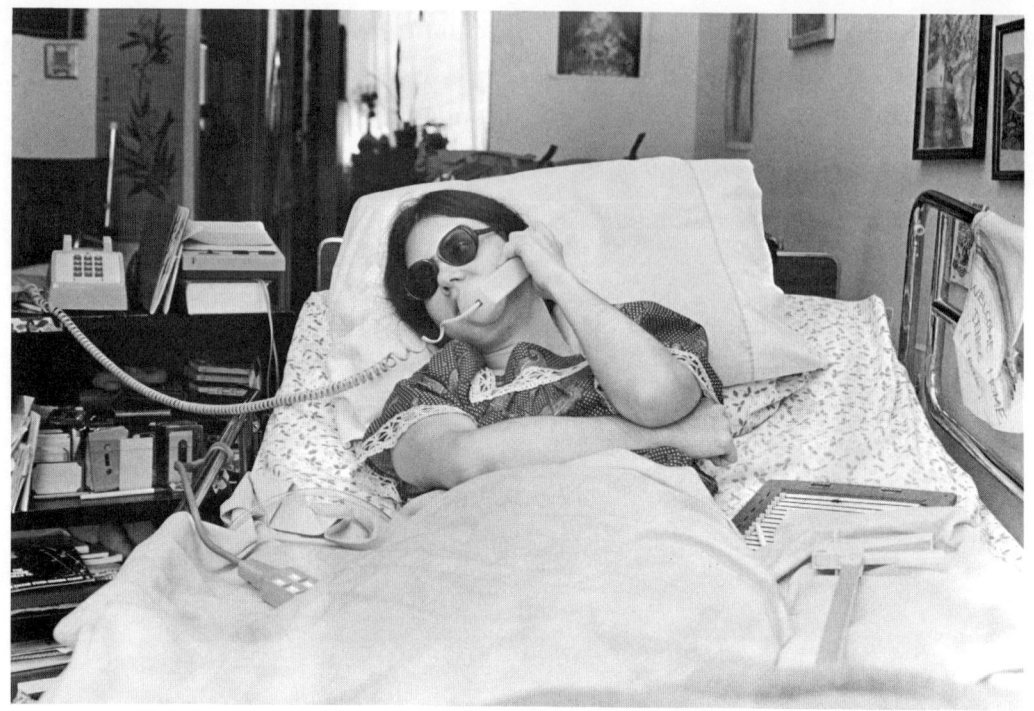

I put something down and cannot find it seconds later.

I no longer cook because I lack both the physical and mental endurance to think through and remember what I'm doing.

I read and comprehend momentarily, but can recall virtually nothing of what I've read.

I think of, remember, or realize something and then, in the same instant, I forget it (for example, remembering someone's name but not long enough to say it).

My short-term memory is poor. If I can hold onto a thought for 30 seconds or more, I'll probably be able to remember it for several minutes, maybe longer. But the first 30 seconds is a no-man's land where thoughts can get hopelessly lost.

My memory for past events is mixed. I can recall, for example, what the practice room for bass players looked like in Baird Hall, but I have a hard time remembering what courses I took in a given year, or what I learned in Baroque Theory.

My long-term memory for events in the recent past is more vague. I forget the details of a meeting two nights ago or the fact that, until the summer of 1981, I awoke in the morning and went to sleep at night, spending very little additional time in bed. When I realized this in February of 1982, it was quite a shock.

I have found that the struggle to overcome some of my disabilities has, at times, been exhilarating or energizing. My struggles with memory loss and fatigue, though, have mostly been just taxing. My extensive use of lists has been a big help, together with the understanding and good humor of those closest to me. But it looks like it's going to be an uphill battle.

How can you prepare for a future in which you may be severely mentally limited? The loss of my vision and my mobility pales when I compare this to the loss of acumen—to be less and less able to read, understand, and follow conversation, to work and to advocate effectively, to participate fully, to remember. All of these are difficulties I have begun to experience. (It's like being under brain arrest.)

I guess I'm already beginning to adapt. Perhaps time, my sense of what needs to be done, and the love, assistance, and support of those closest to me can overcome even this. After all, I've managed blindness and immobility. Like prerequisites to a more advanced course, they have laid much of the groundwork for what may yet come. With faith and hope I carry on . . . remembering to cross MS and memory loss off my list.

To Irene

My best friend is most remarkable. She has congenital deformities of both hands, no intelligible speech, and she functions at a 3- to 4-year level. She is nearsighted, color blind, short statured, and dependent on others for assistance with personal care. She is also black, which many would agree is an additional handicap in today's society.

Yet, after a 3-month vocational training program, and with only a minimum of adaptive equipment, my best friend is now successfully employed in a skilled job that many able-bodied individuals would find daunting.

My best friend's name is Irene. Irene is my guide dog.

She has a black silky coat that looks like it's been polished, and a wonderfully expressive face with big brown eyes that could melt glaciers. Her favorite pastimes are eating, sleeping, playing, and being lovable. Her favorite food is virtually anything organic.

Irene, I am told, is a Greek word meaning peace. My best friend couldn't have a better name.

Irene is loyalty incarnate. She even goes with me into the too-little stalls in public bathrooms. As I write this, she is sleeping in a chair at the foot of my bed. The space is much too cramped for her, but she prefers to stay there, close to me, rather than stretching out comfortably on the double bed or the couch in the other room.

Irene and I have been together for the past 5½-years. Twenty-four hours a day. Seven days a week. We've enjoyed a truly symbiotic relationship.

How does Irene guide me? In the wheelchair I am so close to the ground that I can hold the leather leash very near to her collar. In this way, I'm able to follow her moves without having to hold the metal harness. She, of course, stops for curbs and steps, just as she did when I could walk. But now, in addition, she aims for curb-cuts and driveways.

Oh love of my life, dog of my dreams, hound of my heart. How can I possibly describe this relationship of ours? Should I write of our first week in training school when we were waiting to cross Massachusetts Avenue? You were eager and pulling my arm, but I told you that the light was against us. "Relax," I said. You looked up at me as if to say, "You mean that?" and promptly lay down (in complete disregard of standard guide dog behavior). Or should I tell about the time we went to see the Boston Ballet and you reacted to a bizarre, musically dissonant piece by climbing in terror upon my lap? Or should I write about the 160 or more days we've spent together in various hospitals? How you always knew when to put on the "Lassie act" to impress administrators and Nursing Supervisors.

Remember the time we walked on the subway platform and a disturbed lady greeted us with a cry of "Lord, strike down this demon dog led by a demon!"? Or when you had a gland infection and couldn't wag your tail? Or when you held your ground, even after I'd given the "Forward" command, and saved me from being hit by a car on Newbury Street?

Maybe I should write about how you joyously proceed with choir on Sunday mornings, snore during the sermon, and always know when the worship is over. Or about all the great romps we've had together. (How you love to play and make friends.) Or about how I'm convinced I can tell what you're thinking at any point in time.

I should write about your talent for being able to remember routes we've taken or people we've met only once before. Or about your adaptability in learning to locate curb-cuts, driveways, and elevators. Or your eagerness to shepherd others who travel with me. Maybe I should even mention that I've only run over your paws once in the 2 years I've been in a wheelchair.

I'm so proud of you that I don't care if people stare as we glide together down the street with your leash in my left hand and the wheelchair control in my right.

All in all, you are my pride, my love, and my joy. I can't conceive of life without you. If someone gave me a choice between losing my right arm or losing you permanently, I would part, reluctantly, with my right arm.

But then, what are best friends for?

My Body, My Wimp

Right now it is 8:45 on a Sunday night, and I've been in bed for 5 hours. I want to continue to write, but my body wants to sleep. Can you remember being a little kid and wanting to stay up late, but your mother wouldn't let you? It's frustrating and aggravating to have a mother who never gives in, not even once. Sometimes I want to shout: "I'm 27 years old! Can't I even stay up until 10:00?" But I know from long experience that my protests are of no avail, that my only option is to give in. But not before I negotiate.

"Give me just 20 minutes," I say. "Maybe even 15." I find that I negotiate with my body a lot. "If we go to Jamaica Pond this afternoon and to choir this evening, I promise to stay in all day tomorrow." Or, "I know you're tired, but it's an important meeting, and I really should be there." I even apologize to it: "Chastity (one of my nicknames for my genital area), I'm sorry. Being catheterized is a bitch. What can I say? Let's hope we don't have to do it again for awhile."

For years before it became irrefutably clear that my increasing weakness, fatigue, and pain were the result of illness, I was at war with my body, always pushing it beyond its limits. Now I realize that I treated it like a traitor instead of a besieged ally. I gave it years of grief that it did nothing to deserve.

Time's up. It's 9:00. I got my 15 minutes in. Now I'm negotiating with a body that is busy spacing out. "Let's put the writing board away, take our evening medications, pull up the covers, and go to sleep."

I'll have to leave the lights on since Fred is out. I used to feel badly that I had to trouble someone else to close doors and turn out lights that I couldn't get to. The paradox of their physical closeness and inaccessible distance hit home. Now I rarely think about it. I guess that's adjustment.

It's 9:05, and I'm reluctantly going to sleep. That's adjustment, too. "You know, body," I tease affectionately, "you're really a wimp."

Chapter 2

The Way I See Myself

Don Zimmermann

Let Me Introduce Myself...

My favorite photograph of myself was taken by my father when I was 30 years old. It is a profile, shot from the chest up, clearly showing me sitting on a rock-strewn Maine beach with the pounding surf out of focus in the background. My expression is serious, eyes looking through dark-rimmed glasses to the horizon, thinning hair blowing in the breeze. It's the kind of picture that should appear on the back of my first novel. You know what I mean.

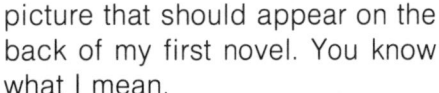

There is no way anyone could know from that picture that I am physically handicapped. My wheelchair was out of sight, and the camera angle was such that it brought no attention to "unusual" parts of my body. Only those who know me intimately would attach any significance to the birthmark visible on my left cheek where, my mother used to explain to me, I was kissed by an angel.

In the photo I am a "normal" human being. It would be nice if society could look at me that way more often. After all, it *is* the way I see myself.

But I know that's an improbable dream.

When I come into a roomful of people, the first thing they notice about me is that I am in a wheelchair, that I am "handicapped." Sure, I'll admit it is the most obvious fact about me, but it is *not* the most important thing to know about me. The worst part about such social experiences is that my wheelchair immediately generates assumptions by the others in the room about what my life must be like. These assumptions are usually totally erroneous and often prevent people from knowing what to say to me. They can't, for example, ask, "What kind of work do you do?" because they assume that someone in my "condition" cannot work. (I am a computer programmer/analyst).

They can't ask, "Are you married?" or "Do you have any children?" because they assume that both of these situations are unlikely, if not impossible, for me to experience. (I was married for 14 years, am currently happily separated, and have three teenage daughters and four older stepchildren.)

They can't ask, "Did you go on a vacation this summer?" because if I don't work, how can I have a vacation? And how could I travel anyway? (I spent 2 weeks in Arizona, highlighted by taking a light plane trip into the Grand Canyon; I've been to Hawaii twice, toured the Canadian Rockies, and visited many parts of the country from Maine to Florida.)

They can't ask, "How did you like driving through that rain (or snow) tonight?" because they assume I can't drive a car. (I've been driving a hand-controlled Dodge van for the last 5 years, getting in and out of it with a hydraulic lift, "Ironsides" fashion.)

They can't ask, "What college did you go to?" because they assume I was lucky if I made it through high school. (I graduated from Wesleyan University in 1957, and went to Graduate School at the University of Illinois.)

The above paragraphs may seem a bit overbearing, but they nonetheless suggest the kinds of thick invisible barriers most people build around themselves with their assumptions and attitudes. I want people to know who I am just as much as they want me to know who they are. Therefore, I usually take the initiative and begin asking them the types of questions they cannot ask me. Then, at the first appropriate moment, I jump right in with something like, "Yes, I know what you mean. I have the same kind of experience in my job."

"Oh, really," they exclaim, relaxing slightly (on newly discovered common ground) for the first time, "what kind of work do you do?"

It's an effective technique. And as the conversation continues, the wheelchair invariably "disappears," or at least fades into the background.

So, what *do* I want people to know about me?

That I am caring toward others, supportive, a good listener, a good friend, and sensitive and responsive to other people's feelings.

That I love seagulls, eagles, and hawks (in that order). That the ocean seems like home. That I sometimes sit so still in the woods that woodchucks pass by me, inches away, unaware of my presence.

That I dream of being a published writer someday—articles, an autobiography, novels (science fiction and otherwise). That I am an effective and entertaining public speaker. That I'm somewhat of a "ham."

That I am a creative and gentle lover. That I love to be loved, too.

That my daughters are the prettiest and most intelligent kids you'll ever meet! That I am objective.

That there is no way I can believe each of us gets only one lifetime to live in this immense universe. That I am sure there is life on other planets.

That I am really proud of my parents, for making the right decisions regarding my upbringing, for giving me independence and a good feeling about myself.

That, though 98 percent of the time I view my "handicap" as an "inconvenience" and seldom allow it to stop me from doing what I want to do or going wherever it is important for me to go, 2 percent of the time I think it's a fucking drag!

That I love Tchaikovsky, Mozart, Beethoven, Elton John, The Eagles, Pink Floyd's "Dark Side of the Moon," Anne Murray, Neil Diamond, Steve and Eydie, Barbara Streisand, and many others.

That I am one helluva good dancer!

That I want peace in the world, and believe it is possible to create it.

That I like who I am and would not want to be anyone else. At least in this lifetime . . .

A Gimp By Any Other Name . . .

"Crippled" is out.

"Disabled" is in. . . . but I don't like it either.

"Handicapped" is old-fashioned, and I accept it easily when labels are necessary. Golfers desire handicaps, eagerly. You can give a horse a handicap, and it can still win the race.

But you know what they do to disabled horses, don't you? *Shoot them!!!*

Actually, the only label I will accept without qualification is "*person!*"

On Crying

I cried when my parents brought me to that "school" for handicapped children in West Virginia, and left me there. I was 4. I don't remember it much.

I cried when I was about to have the first of five surgical operations in 1 year. I was 7. By the fifth surgery it was old hat.

I cried when my parents brought me to a school for cerebral-palsied children and adults in East Hampton, New York, and left me there. I was nearly 10. I was there for 6 years.

I cried when my parents said goodbye at Grand Central Station, as that school migrated to the first of my six winters in Pompano Beach, Florida. I was 10.

I cried when my girlfriend's parents suddenly appeared one Saturday afternoon and yanked her out of the University of Illinois in her senior year because they had heard we were thinking of eventually getting married. They didn't want their "normal" daughter marrying someone with a handicap. I never saw her again. I was 25.

I cried when my lover had to fly back to her home in Michigan after our intensely romantic 63-hour weekend because I knew it meant the end of my shaky marriage. She had repaired my shattered self-image, a beautiful gift, and now I had to act on it. I was 40.

These are the only times in my 46 years that I can remember having cried, sobbing out my sorrow, seemingly out of control. Only six times! I am *not* proud of that.

But, of course, men aren't supposed to cry in our society, especially in my generation and before. We're the "stronger" sex; crying is a feminine weakness. Heaven forbid seeing a man cry! No man wants to be called a "cry baby." Handicapped men especially; we've got to be even stronger than average if we're not to succumb to our difficulties.

Oh sure, I've shed a few tears in between times, over innumerable odd things, like the hostages returning from Iran, the Space Shuttle making its perfect landings, the Mean Joe Green Coke commercial, one of my daughters being temporarily lost for 4 days, seeing starving children cry, Jack Benny and—just lately—Natalie Wood dying, too many movies to mention, the novel *Shogun*, Yul Brynner returning to the "King and I" stage after 30 years, feeling lonely on a Saturday night, etcetera.

But I can't let it loose. So many times I wished I could just let go, and sob my way to some relief. It doesn't happen.

There's no doubt in my mind that there exists a flood of tears dammed up securely deep within me.

Independence versus Vulnerability

In the world of the disabled/handicapped today there are many "buzz words" describing the major concerns: "accessibility," "chair cars," "Section 504," "sexuality attitudinal reassessment," "EEO," "biomedical engineering," and many more. Another that is getting a lot of attention is "independent living." Most of the able-bodied (or temporarily able-bodied) population accepts their state of living independently quite matter-of-factly. Hardly give it a thought. In fact, most of them give it such little attention that they're rather offended if you point out that they are in reality very dependent within their "independence." Dependent on others to grow their food, build their homes, make their clothes, create their entertainment, defend their country, enforce their laws, and a thousand other things.

For the handicapped, "independent living" refers essentially to one concept: being able to live in a "normal" community instead of an institutional environment, to be as productive in "normal" society as possible, to support oneself, if possible, without living off other people's income. In short, to live as "normally" as possible.

Surely, as a teenager, this same motivation was fostered and developed within me. Somehow I always knew I'd grow up, acquire an education, get married (maybe even have kids!), drive a car, get a decent job, live in a "nice part of town," and do all these and other "normal" things. I knew better than anyone that I was just another "normal" person inside this distinctive body, so why couldn't I eventually do all those things? Well, I've done them! And then some.

But over the past few years I've become increasingly aware that, no matter how desirable it is, "independent living" is one of the greatest challenges a person can assume. Like my paycheck in today's economy, it looks good on paper, but living on it every day is often another story.

Independent living is sometimes frightening, dangerous, lonely, frustrating . . .

The "what if's" could drive one nuts:

What if my electric wheelchair breaks down on Saturday night and I can't get it fixed until Monday?

What if I fall out of my chair while emptying the urinal and no one is there to pick me up for hours?

What if my van breaks down on some back country road in zero-degree winter weather?

What if I get diarrhea at my job and everyone knows it?

What if my PCA is in a bad mood or gets sick and doesn't want to or can't help me do something for me?

What if there is a fire in my apartment and I'm alone?

What if . . .

All of these and more are the risks of independent living. They accentuate my vulnerability. Sometimes I'm on terribly thin ice, taking chances that are actually life threatening. Like going out to my van in winter when the temperature is zero or below and the wind is chilling the air to minus 40 degrees or less. I cannot wear gloves as they hamper what limited dexterity I do possess, and I never wear a heavy coat as it would also strain my range of motion. Bare-handed and covered by a couple of wooly sweaters and a Russian-style hat, I face the stinging cold. If I don't get into that van in approximately 2 minutes, I'm in serious trouble: my fingers go numb and refuse to work in their normal fashion, muscles in my arms and shoulders stiffen to near absolute rigidity, and my legs begin to shiver uncontrollably. Add to that the fact that the controls on the electric wheelchair get stiff and difficult to handle in such weather, and you bet I need help . . . quick!

This type of situation can make me feel very fragile and afraid of facing it again. However, my reaction to such experiences, after thanking God for giving me that extra burst of willpower or for sending that helping person along at the right moment, is to ask myself "What can I do to prevent or reduce the chances of that happening again?" Usually, through creative thinking and good planning, I find an answer or two. Like putting my car keys on my lap in a new way so I can grab the right one quicker, or arranging to have someone meet me there to assist, instead of always trying to do it alone.

But regardless of how well I plan, living my life will always involve taking chances, even, at times, risking my life. That's okay with me! Especially when I consider the alternative: *safety*. I could live in the sheltered environment of a nursing home or a state institution where everything is taken care of for me, where I don't have to take any responsibility or make any decisions except which soap opera to watch, and even that might not always be my choice.

No thanks! I'll accept the vulnerability, even when it hurts.

One of the Worst and One of the Best

We all have highs and lows (though it seems that the general public believes the handicapped have only lows; what else could they have in their condition, right?). These ascents toward bliss and descents toward hell frequently teach us more about life and ourselves than does the normal everyday hum of our existence. Two cases in point: first into the pits, then flyin' high!

A couple of years ago, I was Christmas shopping in one of the large indoor malls. As I emerged from Sears, heading into the large central walking area fronting all the other stores, I noticed a large crowd of people clustered around a raised platform. At center stage was a woman, my age, talking to people nearest her, and, because she was using a microphone connected to the mall's loudspeaker system, I soon understood that she was conducting a flower arranging demonstration. Being somewhat curious and liking flowers, too, I drove my wheelchair to the righthand fringe of the crowd and became an observer like everyone else.

The moderator of the show, after explaining some ingenious trick demonstrated by one of her assistants, would then ask the audience a question like: "Which one of you out there has been married the longest?" or "Does anyone of you have a new baby?" She'd then award her latest floral creation to that person(s). After she had done this a couple of times, she suddenly turned in my direction and said, "Oh! There's a man in a wheelchair!"

Like puppets on strings, all 75 plus people turned in my direction to see who she was talking about. I felt like I had instantly been elected Freak of the Week. And then she added, in her most sickeningly sweet voice (close to the microphone so the entire mall could hear), "Would you like some flowers to light up your life?"

I don't know what kept me from exploding, literally! Somehow, I calmly replied, "No, thank you," and whipped my chair into a 180-degree turn and floored it. Writing about this experience even now brings on a heaviness in my chest, but only one-tenth of what I felt then, as I went speeding to the other end of the mall.

How dare that bitch make a spectacle of me! How could she be so goddamn stupid? You know what you can do with your damn flowers, lady? Shove 'em! Why didn't you ask me where my nurse was? Or was that going to be next? Just because I'm in a wheelchair, you assume my life is dreary, sad, and dull; that it needs lighting up. What the hell kind of dim life must you be leading?

These and many more screams rampaged through my head, bringing me as close to going crazy as I'll ever come. A voice within said "Go back there and talk to her," but I knew from the intense choking feeling in my throat that this would be impossible. I decided to cool off first, get something from Brigham's (I was just barely able to utter the words, "Mocha frappe, please."), and try putting myself back together again. One hour(!) later, I returned to speak with the woman, confident that I could maintain my sanity once more. But the flower show was gone!

The next day, when I called the manager of the sponsoring florist, he immediately knew who I was and apologized for the woman's ignorance. I saw her a year later, and sat again in her audience as before. She totally ignored me this time. She must have known I was ready for her.

There have been many lows in my life. Few, though, have contained such a negative mixture of emotions as the flower incident. And there have also been as many, or more, highs. It is difficult to choose only one—my first trip to Hawaii, my high school graduation speech and the reception that followed, the applause of the crowd the first night I did a "stand-up" comedy routine in a Cambridge night club. But certainly of all the highs, becoming a father was a trip and a half!

My wife was 9 days overdue in her pregnancy when she finally decided her labor pains, which she'd already had for 24 hours, were serious enough to warrant being in the hospital. We knew she was going to have twins. As it was her fifth pregnancy (four during her previous marriage), she had realized that *this* one was different. Her abdomen went to basketball size in a hurry. She had played a little badminton in our backyard on her eighth overdue day, thinking, oh why not, maybe it will stimulate the labor. It did.

So, on that ninth day we arrived at the hospital by taxi in the early afternoon. Gail went immediately to the labor room, while I sat in the waiting room. Where I waited. And I waited. I wished I could pace the floor, but since I was in the manual wheelchair (which I cannot push myself), I didn't even have the luxury of wearing out my batteries! Meanwhile, I was getting periodic reports from nurses or Gail's doctor that everything was fine, that nothing much was happening yet. Around 8:00 p.m. the doctor suggested I go home to rest, as she was going to give Gail something to make her sleep through the night to give her strength for the delivery the next day.

I took a cab to a friend's house, slept fitfully, and returned to the hospital by mid-morning. Gail's labor was still mild, even disappearing at times, but the doctor was to induce it at noon. And I waited.

A little after 2 in the afternoon, I heard several nurses rush by the waiting room saying, "The twins are coming!" And then they were gone. All seemed quiet for awhile, hardly anyone in the corridor. Then, again, nurses were passing by in two's and three's, smiling and whispering to themselves and looking purposely at me as they hurried past the doorway. I had the distinct feeling they knew something I didn't, and that it had to do with me!

A few minutes later, Dr. Barnes walked in, smiling the same smile I was seeing on the nurses. She told me I now had two wonderful and healthy

The Way I See Myself

daughters, and my wife was fine. She offered to push me down to the recovery room to see Gail, who looked exhausted but awfully glad it was over.

Through misty eyes, we talked for a few minutes in the hallway; it was one of the happiest moments I can remember, topped off when I first saw my girls after they had been "cleaned up." They looked like miniature versions of Winston Churchill and Nikita Khruschev, but they were beautiful. Wow! I am a father!

Obvious to me now, the serious responsibilities that being a father entails were not foremost in my mind at the moment, nor were the unique problems of being a father in a wheelchair. There was only the glory and the job, and without question the satisfaction of having accomplished something particularly "normal!"

Returning to my job that night (I was then a proofreader in a printing company working the 7 p.m. to 7 a.m. shift 4 nights a week) was a real ego trip, passing out cigars, being asked all kinds of questions, and being kidded about being "double-barreled!"

It surely was an "ordinary moment" for me, and it was great!

A Simple Shtick

For several years now, I guess I've been paraphrasing Teddy Roosevelt's famous motto, for I always roll quietly and carry a moderate-sized stick. Actually, it's just a plain dowel, one-half inch in diameter, and about 24 inches long. It's not tapered or hooked at the ends; it's not decorated or stained with varnish. It's just a white (probably pine) stick that fits neatly in the side of my wheelchair next to the seat cushions.

If you're wondering what my stick is for, you're not the first. People, especially kids, are always asking me about it. "Beating little kids mostly," is one answer I give with a wink, quickly following with some of its real functions. These are:

◇ To push elevator buttons that are too high to reach

◇ To change the thermostat in my apartment

◇ To clean off snow from the outside rearview mirrors on my van

◇ To move things closer to me that are out of my normal reach on the desk, on the coffee table, on kitchen counters, in the bathroom, in my car, in my office

◇ To push down the handle when flushing the toilet

◇ To turn light switches off or on

◇ To pick up my car keys (which are on a keychain that has a leather loop into which the stick fits easily)

- ◇ To align the fly on my pants properly (when necessary) for easier "accessibility" when going to the bathroom
- ◇ To push my roommate's shoes out of my way when they've been left in an inconvenient location
- ◇ To open the refrigerator door
- ◇ To push the door release buzzer in my apartment, letting my guests downstairs into the building
- ◇ To raise and lower the plastic cover of my stereo
- ◇ and dozens more!

Despite the amazing advances in rehabilitative equipment over the last 40 years, innovations that enable people with handicaps to accomplish tasks previously thought impossible, there's nothing like a cheap, readily available, lightweight, easily replaceable when broken, conversation-generating, imagination-stimulating—and simple—shtick!

Words That I Live by . . . or Try To

It seems that approximately once every 10 or 15 years, someone says something to me—or I read in a book—a particular sentence that affects me deeply, uniquely. It becomes etched in my mind, as if in stone, impervious to time. Several of these lines, these mind-carvings, have become vital to my life, messages of "truth" and, more times than I can count, they have helped me set myself back on the right track when I begin to wander or drift.

I offer these to you; perhaps they'll be helpful. Think about them.

The first (pardon the expression) "truth" came from an amazing man who was my principal teacher in all subjects but math at the Carlson's School for Cerebral Palsied Children and Adults. Dr. Theodore Bretscher had a Ph.D. from Columbia University, and he had rather severe cerebral palsy, which made walking a precariously balanced action and affected his speech so much that few people could understand him right away. He should have been teaching at some prestigious college, but I imagine that employer prejudices in the 1930s and 40s were rampant against people with his obvious difficulties.

One afternoon in the one-room Pompano Beach, Florida, schoolhouse, he said to the four or five of us who took our studies seriously:

It is more important to learn how to design a bridge than merely be able to walk across one.

In what context this comment was generated I do not remember, but I do know that it was particularly apropos to me at that time in my life. I was 15 years old, and had recently been informed that I was going to be getting a new set of leg braces to replace the ones I had outgrown. I didn't want them! The pain and discomfort I was experiencing in physical therapy exercises—which were designed to help me "learn to walk"—were not worth the results. After years of practice, I was still unable to walk without having someone hold onto my belt or pants, or without being hung from a "parachute walker." In addition, my ankles produced almost intolerable pain when my feet were twisted in the "proper" or "normal" position to fit into the brace shoes. On my list of priorities, walking was plunging lower each year. With talk of designing bridges, it dropped off the list entirely.

Soon afterward, I phoned my parents (in Connecticut) and told them I didn't want any new braces, and that I wanted to leave Carlson's school when we returned north in the summer to attend a public school and eventually go to college. Their reaction: "We wondered when you'd get that idea, and we're behind you 100 percent!" They were, and I did.

For the next 30 years, physical therapy exercises in general, and walking specifically, were avoided and thought useless. I still think walking is unnecessary in today's world. Oh sure, it would be convenient at times, but since I've even discovered fun ways of dancing in a wheelchair, who needs to walk?

But exercise? That's a different matter. I wish now that I had maintained some form of regular exercise program to improve and stabilize muscle tone in parts of my body that do not normally get much chance to work out. It might also combat that strange urge I occasionally get, that itch to run around the block after a big meal or to run until my body is totally exhausted.

I frequently watch marathon runners—sweating, in pain, sometimes struggling to go another few yards, exhilarated when they've reached their goal—with envy.

Though I try, periodically, to get into the habit of a voluntary exercise program, I've not had tremendous success bucking all those years of physical laziness. But I intend to keep trying. Meanwhile, I have been "designing bridges," and that does feel good. I will also continue doing that.

During the early years of my marriage, when it was becoming terribly obvious that our income was not adequately supporting our expenses, we decided to supplement it by becoming active in the "soap business" as Amway distributors. My wife's sale of 200 pounds of bleach and detergent to the aircraft carrier USS Essex (now in mothballs) was the highlight of our career. But pregnancy with our twins delayed further sudsy activity until a year later when we signed up with a newer, "more promising" home care products company called Bestline—a "ground-floor opportunity." Despite a couple of very active years in the business involving much travel and considerable overhead expenses, we never really got off that ground floor. It's debatable whether we even broke even, and, in the long run, it didn't help our marriage. But now, looking back, what we earned was not nearly as valuable as what we learned.

As part of the sales training for the soap business, we were provided with several self-improvement books designed to help us achieve a positive mental attitude. One of the best of these was Napoleon Hill's *Think and Grow Rich*. "Rich" was not restricted to its usual monetary reference; it applied also to internal/spiritual and to self-image "richness." It was through this book that I first became aware of the concept that "thoughts are things," and that what you most think about *will happen*. We create our own realities!

It was an alarming concept, at first, one which initially generated a natural skepticism. But, in the years since discovering it, I have come to accept it totally. I am where I am today because of my past and current *thoughts*, and so, I believe, is everyone else.

If I thought of myself as an unfortunate person burdened by a "severe physical handicap," if I believed my life must be one of seclusion and isolation because the world does not accept handicapped people as equals to the "normal," if I allowed architectural barriers to stop me from going where I wanted, if I felt the world owed me something and I decided to wait for it . . . if these were a sample of my most frequent thoughts, I would certainly not be where I am today. And, though I have been fortunate that key people in my life have helped to instill positive thoughts in me, I believe that even they (the people) would not have been a part of my reality if I had allowed that reality to be a negative one.

I am responsible for my current reality; you are responsible for yours. Meditate on that one periodically. To me, it's a lifesaver.

Additionally, one sentence from Hill's book remains cerebrally etched within me:

Every adversity carries within it the seed of an equivalent or greater benefit.

I believe it. But I had to think back on my life to test the idea.

The most obvious "adversity" in my life, my physical handicap, has brought me and my parents (and even my close friends) experiences, feelings, and knowledge that might not have been realized without it. The adversity of a failed marriage has taught me what qualities are crucial in an intimate long-term relationship and in all my interactions with others. The adversity of a low-paying, dull career as a proofreader many years ago produced the right experiences and connections with people that led me to a data processing career that pays well and, more importantly, that I enjoy 90 percent of the time. The adversity of being in the soap business led me to philosophies, concepts, and thoughts that have been keys to the success of my life so far. And it goes on.

The title of Ram Dass' first book, *Be Here Now*, has done more for me than any other title or most other books. I have spent more time with and have obtained more value from those three words than from any other words in our language. Here, briefly, is what they mean to me:

BE: *To exist as a whole person as completely as possible throughout all experiences of my life, bringing the full extent of my positive energies to every activity.*

HERE: *In this place (in front of my typewriter). Wherever I happen to be is here*; *it is the only place in which I can make things happen for sure. Oh, I may be able to influence what happens in other places,* there, *but not with the same confidence and surety as* here.

NOW: *At this particular moment, right now. Not in the past, for it is gone, done, over, cemented in time. Not in the future, for I do not know what it contains. The only time I can do anything about is* now; *I can waste it by being lazy, or I can put all my energies into this moment, whatever I am doing. The latter option is much more satisfying than the former.*

Combine these three words with what Stewart Emery said in his book, *You Don't Have to Rehearse To Be Yourself*:

Life is simple, but it isn't easy.

Emery was referring to choices. One of the simplicities of life is the truth that if you are "being here now," you will realize that you *always* have a choice of what you can do in the "now." Making a choice and acting on the decision you've made is the not-so-easy part, but the choices are always there. If you don't like the way things are "now," see your choices and act on the ones you feel best about.

An honest admission: I don't always live up to these words. Sometimes I forget, and things begin going bad. Fortunately for me, the bad times keep getting shorter and shorter the older I get, probably because I don't have to remember these positive and basic "truths" as much as before.

They are a part of me.

From Lizard Head Rock

Gray Mountain is located on the norther edge of West Sedona, Arizona. About two-thirds of the way down its western crest is a large rock that juts out, a carved profile of a massive lizard's head with a strong flat jaw.

Beneath the overhanging jaw sits a tall man who never moves. He is shaded by the rock throughout most of the day, and is bathed in the light of the setting sun before darkness makes him disappear.

He is totally undisturbed, totally at peace with himself. Material possessions mean nothing to him. Though he would not object to being visited,

he needs no one else to feel whole. He is connected to the earth and knows he is a part of the heavens.

I know the man. I can become him merely by closing my eyes, seeing what he sees, feeling what he feels.

It does not matter that, in other people's realities, the man is nothing more than a juniper tree.

Chapter 3

Being Deaf and Surprised

Nancy V. Becker

Not a Spelling Mistake

Deaf. With a "d" it describes a condition. With a "D" it describes a culture.

When I was born, my hearing was fine. At age 2, I became deaf. At age 16, I became Deaf.

If you're a bit confused by this distinction, don't worry. It's a pretty new idea. I'm still confused by it sometimes, too.

The Cowboy, the Mouse, and Me

As a child, I was lonesome much of the time. There I was, a fat, deaf kid with buck teeth; an easy target for the other kids to make fun of—and every chance they got, they did.

I knew they were putting me down, taking advantage of me, thinking of me as pretty much nothing. But because speech, for me, was difficult, I was unable to taunt them back. I didn't understand then why they treated me so differently; I just knew that I wasn't the happiest kid around.

I so much wanted them to notice me instead of me always noticing them. I can remember once standing out in the middle of the street with the cars zooming by and all the kids looking on. This was my way of saying, "You think I'm nothing, huh? Well, watch this."

Not too smart, I guess. Not even too successful. They made fun of me even more.

Some mornings I would tell my mother that I was sick, and that I wouldn't be able to go to school. I was lying, of course. Fact was, I didn't want to face those kids on the street again. It was a pretty good strategy for awhile, until my mother decided to call the doctor to find out what was really wrong with me. I made an instant recovery.

I'm sure my mother always knew that I was lying about being sick, but I doubt she ever really understood why. I'm not sure that she ever knew how I felt about not fitting in, about not belonging with the kids on the street.

Because I had almost no one to talk to, I'd talk to myself. Or I'd talk to the wall or to the mirror. I was watching myself, my face, to see how I looked when I tried to talk. Did I look like my father? My mother?

But it was really the TV that I talked to the most. I remember wondering what it was that Roy Rogers was talking about, and then deciding that what-

---

Editor's Note: As Nancy points out, English is not her first language. American Sign Language is. Consequently, her writing, while clear and fully comprehensible, contains errors in grammar and syntax that may distract certain readers from the substance of her communication.

For this reason, Nancy's chapter does not read exactly as it was originally written. The writing has, for lack of a better term, been interpreted from her original text.

I have tried to keep the meaning and tone of Nancy's words just as she intended. She, of course, has reviewed and approved each successive draft.

ever it was, I could make up just as good a story. And I did. With my holster securely fastened, I created scenes and speeches. Or I'd follow Roy's mouth movements and try to imitate what I thought might be going on.

Then, when it was time for Mickey Mouse, there I'd be with my ears on. It made little difference to me that I had no idea what the show was about; it became my show soon enough. And on my show, nobody ever made fun of me.

Mouth Flap

My mother remembers when I was still able to hear. I was about 2 years old. She tells me that I could say three words: "milk," "cookie," and "apple." Then the high fever made me deaf. I didn't talk again until I went to school.

The first school I attended was strictly oral; all the kids there were deaf, and we were all expected to learn to speak. It was at this school that I began the continually frustrating process of learning to read lips and to make sounds—sounds I would never hear.

I'm proud of the speech and lipreading skills that I learned; they've helped me to get along in the hearing world. But the focus only on oralism was wrong.

No one there ever taught me—or even talked to me—about the Deaf world. My world. To them, it was only important that I speak.

Signing was not allowed, so we all learned it informally from each other. We picked it up quickly and signed all the time on the sly.

After school, the deaf boys from a neighboring school would come and wait for us by the window of our classroom. Once, just before the teacher returned to dismiss us, I was signing to one of the boys outside. Naturally, the Assistant Superintendent chose that moment to drop in. I felt the sharp whack on the back of my head; there hadn't been enough time for anyone to warn me to "shut up my hands."

The Assistant Superintendent was furious at me for using sign language. My language.

I remember one math class that was particularly frustrating and painful for me. The teacher had spent the entire time trying to teach me *how to pronounce* a specific math term. I don't remember what the word was, but I'm sure I never said it perfectly. I do remember that I learned no math that day.

Another day, my English teacher and I got into a difficult argument. Being the student, I, of course, lost. Without using my voice, I mouthed the words, "I hate you," never dreaming that the teacher would see. And even if she did, I was sure she wouldn't understand.

She did see. And she understood perfectly.

After school, I reported to her office and waited for what would certainly be a terrible punishment. Instead, she entered smiling and told me that she wanted to be my friend. This was the first time a teacher had ever crossed the teacher-student barrier and expressed extra warmth and concern. I was so pleased. My friendship with that teacher is one of the memories I most cherish from my years at the oral school.

Today, when people ask me whether I think deaf kids should learn to speak, I answer that I don't want to see any deaf kid trying to flap his mouth around, trying to say something that probably won't be understood anyway.

In my opinion, deaf kids should be taught sign language first; it's a language that will *work* for them. Only *after* they know sign language would it make sense to see if they can learn to speak. And if they can't, then they shouldn't be forced.

Teaching speech to a child who will never talk makes absolutely no sense. It's just a frustrating waste of time for everyone, time that could be better spent focusing on that child's general education.

Nothing, Dear

I'm often asked how I feel about being deaf. It's not an easy question to answer because sometimes I feel handicapped being deaf, sometimes I don't. When I want to make a phone call, for example, I'm reminded that I'm deaf. I'm handicapped. Or when I'm with a group of people who are chatting away, then, too, I'm reminded. They can't be expected to stop their conversation every other minute to make sure I understand everything being said.

Then there are all those basic problems of living that also remind me that I'm deaf: when something goes wrong with the electricity or the plumbing or the car. I'd love to be able to communicate with the people who help me solve these problems; I want to talk with them, find out what they're doing, learn what I might be able to do by myself the next time the problem occurs. But you won't find many people who'll take the time to pass notes back and forth.

There was one man, though, a plumber, who I'll never forget. He was willing to write things down for me, but he was Greek. We were stymied until we tried communicating with gestures we made up on the spot. He was so patient. Our mime show was a great success for both of us.

Another time, a different plumber came over, and he, too, was very patient. He looked right at me and spoke slowly so that I could read his lips. Still, I couldn't understand what he was trying to tell me. He repeated what he said, and I still couldn't make sense of it. Frustrated, I ran downstairs and asked one of my hearing friends to help me.

My friend came up and, as soon as she heard what the plumber had to say, she turned to me and finger-spelled "s-t-u-t-t-e-r." No wonder my lipreading didn't work. As far as I was concerned, this plumber, too, might as well have been speaking Greek.

I often get frustrated when I watch television and will call my hearing friends (those who have a TTY) to see if they can help me understand. This is particularly true when it looks like an emergency of some kind is being described.

Three years ago, we had a huge blizzard. I learned afterwards that everyone had known it was coming but me; I didn't know about it at all until it was on me.

When I was a child, I went to the same summer camp for 11 years in a row. I was the only deaf camper there for all that time, and, often, I was reminded of it. At group meetings, I would go outside to play by myself, something that the counselors encouraged. They couldn't see a way to have me participate. Of course the other kids picked up on this and figured there was nothing wrong with leaving me out of many of their games. I was deaf. I was an outsider. I was somebody you made exceptions for, somebody you made excuses for.

Even around my family table, I was frequently made to remember that I was deaf. Because of the philosophy at the oral school, my parents never learned to sign. So, when we wanted to communicate, we wrote notes or talked very slowly to each other. A lot of patience was required from both sides making this kind of communication painfully frustrating.

Someone, for example, would tell a joke. Everybody but me would laugh. "What was it?" I'd ask.

"Nothing, dear," they'd say. I was furious.

"That's not fair," I explained. "I can't read so many lips all at the same time."

"That's okay, dear. It was really nothing." If someone did decide to repeat for my sake, the new version always seemed a lot shorter.

Often, of course, I knew it was more than nothing. How could everything around me—things that others in the family would talk about at length—be "nothing?"

When my grandfather died, for example, I wasn't living at home. I wasn't told about it until months after he was buried. Similarly, when one of my mother's close friends passed away—a man who had been wonderful to me—I didn't find out about it until I caught a casual remark made at dinner *several years later.*

These kinds of things, these kinds of reminders, have occurred to me all my life. They're something I've gotten used to, something I can't stand.

Frenzy

When I was 11, my mother, my stepfather, and I went to Cuba for a vacation. My mother was pregnant with my sister at the time.

Cuba was beautiful; I was having a wonderful time. Then, one morning my mother said we had to stay together and be very careful. We couldn't go outside, she said—not for food, not to find my new friends, not at all. She didn't tell me why. In the lobby of our hotel, I saw soldiers. I thought they were planning to kill my mother's baby.

Our plane tickets had been taken away by Cuban officials, but my stepfather managed to find three more. We rushed to the airport to fly home. I was confused by the frenzy, but no one had time to explain things to me now.

At the airport, a customs official started talking to me quickly. I could only understand that he was asking me questions; I didn't know what he wanted to know. I was frightened. I couldn't read his lips. I nodded my head at everything he said.

Suddenly, my mother interrupted. "No, no. She's deaf. She was born in the United States." Then she looked at me and asked, slowly and clearly, "Were you born in the United States?"

"Yes," I answered, "in Brooklyn." The customs official waved us on.

In school the next day, no one believed that I had been in Cuba. I wondered why. It wasn't until some years later that I learned about Castro and about the revolution that began during my vacation.

From deaf to Deaf

At 16, I went to a school where signing was allowed. My life changed drastically. I made real friends at this new school, friends that I could talk with. I was amazed at how easily I could be understood, at how easily I could understand.

My new language changed my life. At age 16, I went from being deaf to being Deaf.

Music to My Eyes

When I was a child, my mother so much wanted to believe when I told her that I could hear a little. It didn't matter to her that what I was "hearing" were only vibrations.

I took piano lessons for a full year. Then, for another year, I took lessons on the recorder. In one case I memorized which keys to press. In the other, I memorized which holes to cover. In each case the teacher would tell me if I was playing correctly or not. In both cases, I learned nothing. Of course.

These two failures made me hate music and anything that I thought was even closely related to it, like poetry or dancing. I simply avoided anything musical.

Then, not too long ago, a friend offered to interpret a song for me. I was naturally skeptical, but because she was so excited, I decided to go along. First, she gave me the words to read. Then she signed them, integrating the song's rhythm with American Sign Language. It was beautiful to see. I began to reconsider what music might offer to me, what messages songs might have for me.

Now I spend several evenings a year at interpreted concerts. I've even been known to step onto the dance floor once in awhile, too.

Whose Mainstream?

Everyone talks a lot about mainstreaming today. It's a good thing, they say. People with disabilities should be mainstreamed, they say. I say differently, at least as far as deaf children are concerned. I'm against deaf kids being mainstreamed. Let me tell you why.

I always went to schools for the deaf. My peers were always deaf, but not my teachers. In fact, until I was 16, I had never seen a deaf professional.

At Gallaudet, the only liberal arts college for deaf people, I received my BS degree. There, too, all the students, (and some of the faculty) were deaf. The class president: Deaf. All the school officials: Deaf. I was the Secretary for Athletic Affairs: Deaf. When we held social events: Deaf. Sororities: Deaf.

All the help we might need we could get from Deaf others, and this is so important. A Deaf person is the only one who really knows how to help another Deaf person. A hearing person knows how to take over, not how to help. A hearing person assumes that when a Deaf person asks for help, then that person is admitting that the task—whatever it is—is too difficult. Taking over replaces helping. There's no challenge left.

At Gallaudet, we all helped each other; there was plenty of challenge to go around. When one of us asked for help, that's what was offered.

Maybe hearing people just don't know how to help. Maybe they think they're being kind by taking over. They just don't know how important the difference is. (Let me share a little secret with you. Sometimes when a hearing person offers to help and the deaf person knows that helping means taking over, that's very easy to take advantage of. Think about that the next time someone asks for your help.)

Then, of course, deaf people can be easily fooled by hearing people. There are so many parts of the world that deaf people just don't know about, so many parts that they're afraid to face. They haven't learned about the world as easily or as naturally as hearing people have. So they feel at a disadvantage.

The point is, there are just so many more opportunities in which deaf kids can become involved at a school for deaf children. At a public school, just like at my summer camp, the teachers may not know how to include deaf kids. Or else including the deaf kids becomes such a big deal that the deaf kid is made to feel too special. As a result, the deaf kid in the mainstreamed school finds that the number of opportunities available to him or her is limited. There are no such limits in a school for the deaf. There's nothing special about the deaf kids being involved in everything. In my opinion, that's just how it should be.

Now maybe for some deaf kids, being in a mainstreamed school represents an important challenge. "I can do it," they say to themselves. "I can show off in the hearing world."

But often, when these same kids come to visit a school for the deaf, they suddenly wake up to all that they've been missing. They see a whole new range of opportunities that were never available to them in the place where they went to show off. They realize that they weren't challenged; they were limited.

Maybe I'd feel differently about all this if I had gone to a mainstreamed school myself. I'm willing to think that I might. But I doubt it.

An Editorial Sign

The sign for the word "mainstreaming" is, like many signs, smooth, graceful, and flowing. With palms down, one hand rests on the other with the fingers of each interlocked and pointing straight ahead; in this position, the hands glide forward from the chest.

Deaf friends of mine who are teachers in mainstreamed schools use a version of this sign that tells you very clearly how they feel about deaf kids being placed in public schools. In their version, the interlocking fingers are not pointing straight ahead; instead, they're bent and twisted as if they were falling all over each other, getting in each other's way. No two fingers are headed in the same direction, and in this position the two hands move slowly, unsteadily forward.

No "Nothing"

Some deaf children believe that deaf people die immediately after graduation from high school; they're not used to seeing older versions of themselves. I, for some reason, knew I would grow older, but I never considered my future very much. I wasn't sure what there was to consider. I never knew, for example, that I could become a teacher. As I mentioned, I had never even seen a Deaf professional until I was 16 years old.

During my college days at Gallaudet, a Deaf friend invited me to her home in Michigan. I had gone on visits like this many times, but this one would be different: both my friend's parents were Deaf, and her hearing sister was a fluent signer. That's how they communicated! Freely. Openly. Without struggling to be understood.

This was the first Deaf family I had ever spent time with, and for me the experience was like entering into an entirely new world. I was in awe as I watched them talk with each other. How easy it was. How simply curiosities were satisfied. There was no stopping for exaggerated mouth movements, no writing notes. No one said, "It was nothing, dear."

Last year I was a bridesmaid at my brother's wedding. The entire ceremony was interpreted. It was such a beautiful and happy ceremony . . . for everyone.

Being Deaf . . . and Surprised

If I'm talking with someone and the person should look away, I'll figure that he or she was bored. Worse, I might think that what I said was offensive.

For when two Deaf people talk to each other, they look at each other all the time. If one of them is going to look away, he'll first tell the other, "Wait a minute. I'm looking away now." Then, when he looks back, the two can continue to talk and no one's feelings were hurt. (Of course, if the one who looked away should forget to look back, then the other person will feel pretty insulted.)

It's easy for Deaf people to get embarassed at a dance; they can't hear the music. So, for example, they might be dancing out on the floor with everyone else when, suddenly, the music ends. Song's over. Everyone else stops moving around. But not the Deaf people. They just keep on dancing . . . until they look around. Then they stop real quickly.

Deaf people don't need music to dance.

When Deaf people get excited, they tend to nudge each other. It's just like a hearing person saying to a friend, "Hey. HEY!"; it's a way of showing a lot of emotion. Sometimes, though, like anyone else, a Deaf person can get really carried away with strong feelings. When that happens, you might have to step away to avoid getting bruised.

Deaf people often learn about everyday things through trial and error. That means that sometimes they don't learn at all.

It was only very recently, for example, that I learned about this thing called an IRA account. I immediately rushed out to share the news of this new and interesting program with my hearing friends. How surprised I was when they told me that IRAs weren't new anymore, that the many different programs have been around for awhile. It's almost as if they were saying, "Where have you been?"

This kind of experience happens to me and to my Deaf friends often. Another example: When I was a young student, I rode the same train to and from school every morning and afternoon. On one of the coldest days of the year, with the snow blowing all around, I boarded that train and settled in for the familiar ride home. But I quickly discovered that the train was heading somewhere else; it was taking a route I had never seen before. I was nowhere near my neighborhood.

I scribbled a note to the conductor: "Isn't this the train to Tarrytown?"

He wrote back: "Guessed you missed the schedule change. It was announced over the loudspeaker just before we left the station."

I was never taught such basic things as how to open a bank account, how to fill out income tax forms, how to get insurance. I wasn't even taught that such things existed. It was the same with sex. Sex education for deaf people didn't exist. Like every other Deaf person, I learned about sex from the gossips and big talkers in school. And, like most deaf people, I learned about it all wrong.

You might think that I could learn about anything at all simply by reading through books, newspapers, and magazines. But when I try to read, I often get frustrated. English, you must understand, is my second language; I have to read so slowly. It's a struggle for me to understand.

If I lived with a hearing roommate, and if that roommate were willing to share things with me, I might learn about many of these everyday things a lot sooner. But by living alone and socializing mostly with Deaf friends, I often wind up feeling left a little bit behind.

Being surprised is a big part of being Deaf.

Noisy Silence

Once, when I was a house parent in a program for deaf children, a hearing friend came to stay in one of the spare rooms. She was a teacher and had brought with her some reports to work on. After she had been in the house just a short while, she came to my room and said, "This place is too quiet. You have a radio or something that I could borrow?"

"But the radio makes noise," I answered. "Won't it disturb you?"

"Not at all," she said. "I'll feel safer, more comfortable, having it on."

I didn't understand what she meant. "Do hearing people have to have sounds around them all the time?" I asked.

"I do," she answered.

How different that is for deaf people. In fact, it's practically the opposite. When a deaf person is working at something, concentrating hard, and another person starts tapping away or banging on something, the deaf person will ask them to stop. The vibrations are too distracting.

They Ask

In recent years, I have been invited frequently to speak with public school children about my experiences as a Deaf person. I consider this kind of communication crucial, and I love doing it. The kids always ask a wide range of good questions, the kind I wish had been asked years ago. And answered.

They ask, for example, "Can deaf people drive?"

I show them my car keys, then I let them in on a little secret. Deaf people, I tell them, are often better drivers than hearing people. They have no radios, no other sounds, to distract them.

They ask, "Can deaf people talk on the phone?"

I show them my portable TTY which allows me to communicate with anyone else who has one. I show them how it works, and we play with it together.

They ask, "How do you hear the alarm or the doorbell?"

I introduce them to Luke, my dog, and explain about hearing ear dogs. I show them the flashing light on my alarm clock and describe the system in my home that causes lights to flash when the doorbell or the phone rings or when the smoke alarm goes off.

They ask, "Do you ever watch television?"

I tell them about my decoder which provides captions for a number of shows. I tell them being deaf is expensive.

They ask, "Can deaf people get married? Can they have babies? Will the babies be deaf, too?"

I tell them about my Deaf friends who are married and who have both deaf and hearing children.

They ask, "Can deaf people hear anything at all?"

I show them my hearing aid and explain how the vibrations change when I'm wearing it. I tell them that what a deaf person hears is different for each deaf person.

After their questions, we practice reading each other's lips so they'll appreciate how difficult this skill is. Then my interpreter and I will sign for a short while without using our voices; this lets the kids get a tiny dose of what it feels like to be left out. Then I'll tell them a couple of Deaf jokes and explain a little about our Deaf culture; kids are always curious to know the rules. So I tell them it's okay to tap a Deaf person to get his or her attention, and that it doesn't help to scream.

I also tell them that it's easy to become friends with a Deaf person simply by learning a few signs and then relying on mime and talking slowly. Before I leave, I make sure they know that, in fact, they already have one Deaf friend. And they do.

Easier Said Than Signed

Deafness is not something that someone else can see right away, so it often happens that strangers will have no idea that I can't hear them. When they find out, though, they suddenly act very differently. They want to pity me.

That's their problem, I figure, not mine.

Not long ago, an older woman came up to me while I was shopping and began talking to me; I think she was asking me questions. I just looked at her and smiled. Finally, I said "Hello" and went on about my business. While I continued to shop, the woman continued to watch me until she approached again and began once more to talk.

"Wait a minute," I said. "I can't hear you. I'm deaf. But I can read lips, if only you'll talk slower . . . "

"Oh," she said, "I'm so sorry." And again she walked away, this time for good.

Trying to talk with the hearing world can be a real challenge; the people in it seem always so impatient. I want to say, "Come on. Try it again. Tell me. Don't just give up. Let's write it down on paper. Let's communicate." But for most people, I suppose, that's easier said than signed.

Hearing people smile at me a lot when they learn that I'm deaf. Their smiles, though, aren't smiles of happiness.

Hearing People Hear Hearing People

I find that it's easy and too common for the talents and contributions of Deaf people to go unrecognized and unappreciated. Say, for example, that a Deaf person and a hearing person are both staff in a program for deaf children. Assume, too, that the administrator of the program does not know sign language (this is not uncommon, by the way). Now the two staff persons work together to develop terrific new ideas for their program. Naturally these ideas will be communicated to the administrator by the hearing staff member. Who do you suppose will get the credit?

I'm not even suggesting that the hearing person tries to take the credit for himself. But since he's the one to talk—and since the one he's talking to is hearing—won't he be the one seen as responsible for the good ideas?

This example may seem trivial to some; I raise it, though, to make my point as clearly as I can. In the world of the hearing, Deaf people are often forced to wonder: Who get's the credit?

And who gets overlooked?

Just One Thing

I won't let my deafness stop me. Why should it? So far, there's only one thing I'm *sure* I'll never do: I'll never hear again. Just one thing.

Now that's not so bad, is it?

Chapter 4

My Body Is New to Me Again

Debbi Talshir

I had always been proud of my legs. They were strong and shapely, so good for the sports I was good at. So when the numb feelings first began, I rubbed and slapped at them, trying to wake them from what I wanted to believe was a momentary sleep. They didn't rouse.

I tried health food for awhile. Then mind control. Still the numbness continued.

Night after night I prayed for my legs. Please, God. Don't take them away.

They went anyway. And I entered a new realm of existence.

I was 25 years old, a musician and a nurse. Recently separated and with a newborn son, I was certain that life held only the promise of good things.

I was 25 years old . . . and I started getting dizzy. That's how my MS began.

In the summer of 1977, while the dizziness continued for 5 straight months, I endured what seemed like every conceivable test known to modern medicine. Finally I was informed of my diagnosis: multiple sclerosis, a deterioration of the insulation around certain nerves.

My training as a nurse had taught me what MS means—for other people. Now, the other person was me. Suddenly I was the patient, and I had to have the answer to one question: What's going to happen to me now?

No one would answer me. Not the doctors. Not the nurses. Not the social workers. I was told nothing. I was just left alone to be dizzy and, naturally, to assume the worst.

In the summer of 1977, I felt my fright might kill me. Five years later, the hurt remains.

By the spring of the following year my legs became noticeably weaker. I could still walk with some difficulty, but the strength in my lower legs was clearly giving out. By the next winter I had to use a wheelchair. And that's when the culture shock began.

In the wheelchair I was treated as though I could not think, hear, speak, or move. To most people I became a non-person.

Earlier in my life, I had been a direct care nurse giving help to people with physical problems. Today, I'm the one with the physical problems. I'm the one who, on occasion, needs some help. I've discovered how much harder it is to get it than to give it.

My Body Is New to Me Again

Where once I was a part of the medical profession, today I'm apart from it. Where once I was so valued for belonging to it, today I'm frustrated for needing it.

To me the irony is enlightening and pathetic.

First in my life is a little guy named Ben. He's 6 years old. He's my son. And he's my buddy. In his words: "We look after each other." Ben's father and I separated almost immediately after Ben was born.

When I conceived, carried, and gave birth to Ben, I was unaware that MS was less than 3 years away. I was free to think only about being a responsible and loving parent. MS hasn't altered that freedom a bit. Fact is, today I'm amused by people who wonder how Ben has grown to be so healthy and so happy, how he's become such a fun, giving, confident—sometimes bratty—individual. In their eyes, I guess the successful parent must be able to run with her child.

It was early spring 1979 when I came to accept that my legs had grown too weak to carry me around any longer. And there, at the end of the hall amidst boxes of household miscellany, stood (sat?) my new motorized wheelchair. Ben and I were still in the process of moving into our latest apartment, and he had already asked, several times, what the wheelchair was going to be like. It was the same question I had been asking myself. This shiny contraption had only arrived this morning; I was as confused about it as my son, then 3 years old.

Here was a little boy, in many ways just starting his life. And here was his mother, doing pretty much the same. I didn't know how to answer his questions . . . or my own.

It had been my friend, Ed, who convinced me that the wheelchair would be necessary; it represented, he explained, the only way I'd be able to travel at a reasonable rate. Ed, seated in his own wheelchair, spoke with authority.

Still I had my doubts and my fears. How was I going to drive this thing? What if it breaks down. And what about Ben? He was only used to a mother who was tall and who walked.

Ed arrived to find me staring at the chair and invited (more correctly, he ordered) me to take a drive with him, then and there. "Come on," he said, without a hint of concern, "we're going to the river."

"But the cars," I protested, "They'll never see me. And anyway, I don't know how to handle this thing. I'll die out there . . . sitting down."

Ed just laughed as I tried to beg off, and he repeated his invitation firmly, "Just follow me," he breezed. "It'll be a cinch." I hesitated. "Get your ass in that chair now!" he screamed. Ed's not a screamer. So I sat.

There we were, Ed and I, a mini-convoy heading onto the streets of downtown Boston. The lead driver up front was silent. The student, behind, couldn't keep her mouth shut. Ben walked alongside.

The river was only five city blocks from my apartment, and I was whining and complaining every inch of the way. At the first intersection, I jiggled to a less than graceful stop and paused for a settling deep breath.

Each street was a raceway, fast and full and frightening. Without thinking, I scooped Ben into my lap; this was the seasoned mother acting, not the novice crip.

As the convoy started up again, Ben squealed with delight, obviously enjoying the ride. His comfort comforted me. And, though I still managed not to miss one pothole en route, we arrived much more smoothly, much more certainly than we had departed.

That was 3 years ago, and I've been zooming around in this chair ever since. I've learned how to change its parts and check its air pressure. I've learned how to carry a child on it, mostly my own, sometimes others'. I've learned how to negotiate the obstacles of the city.

Some people go for walks in their spare time. I go for 7-mile-an-hour rides. I feel like I'm in a ski lift that doesn't ever go up.

Our bodies are so delicate. It amazes me, sometimes, that they ever work at all. Extraordinary machines.

So why is it that most people never give their bodies a second thought? Why is it that to them a body is just there?

Unless, of course, something goes wrong with it. Then it isn't all just there anymore, and the same person who never thought about it before now can't stop doing only that.

Why should it take a loss to make that gain in appreciation?

I was used to dressing a body almost 6 feet tall that walked. And that looked good.

Now I clothe a shorter body that sits. But it will look good, too . . . with a little planning and a lot of trial and error.

My body is new to me again. And no one teaches you how to dress it for sitting.

Ben and I were ending a long afternoon walk, and I could see that he was beginning to tire. We were stopped at a busy intersection, Ben holding onto the arm of my chair; I picked him up and put him on my lap.

My Body Is New to Me Again

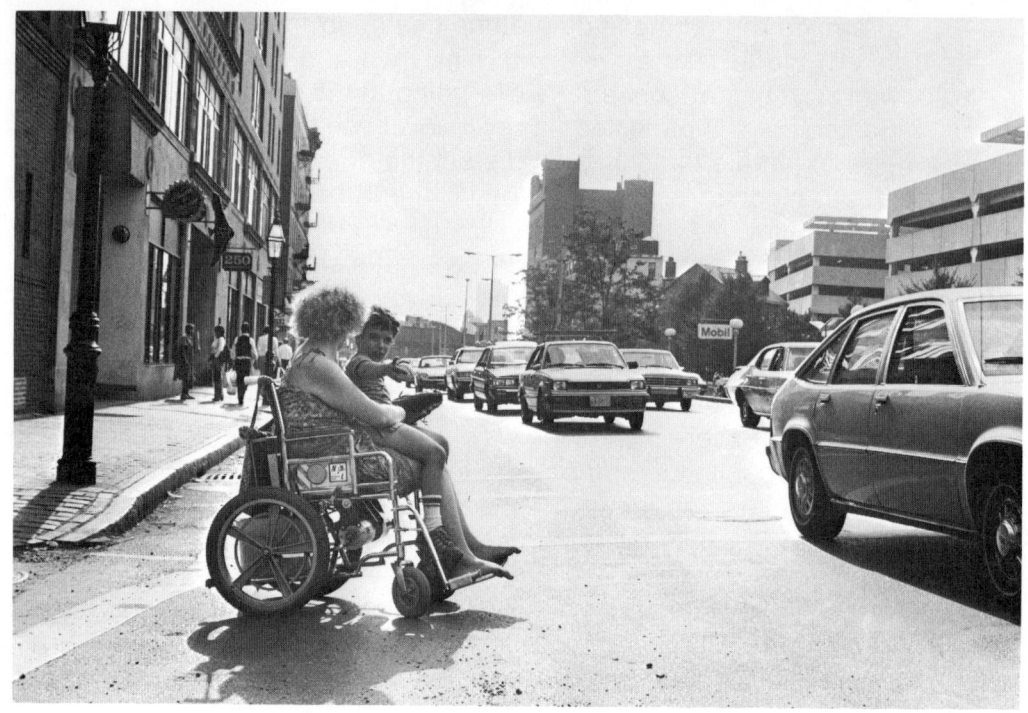

A passerby was witnessing this brief scene with interest, and, as we began to move, she approached, "He's quite a handsome young man," she said. "Are you taking him home to his mother?"

"She *is* my mother," Ben answered.

"No," I followed, "just taking him back to Child World where I rented him for the afternoon."

In retrospect, I'm aware that Ben's response was a lot more correct, a lot more adult, than my own. But I was angry at the intrusion and had to strike back at the ignorance that accompanied it. I should have been more patient, more understanding. I usually am. But it's wearing being a full-time street educator; its damn annoying to have to be rearranging the attitudes of others all the time.

The assumptions and prejudgments of others are, without question, the most difficult obstacles I face. And I face them—Ben and I face them—every single day.

Even now, when I come home with a new pair of shoes, Ben will ask: "This means you can walk again, doesn't it?"

Outwardly, I answer him honestly. "There's no magic in shoes," I tell him. "Shoes can't make me walk."

Inwardly I want to agree with him so much.

One late afternoon, I was sitting on the floor of my apartment waiting for Kathy, a friend of a friend, to drop by. Thirty minutes later, the two of us must have looked like the best of pals—gabbing, laughing, getting a new friendship quickly off the ground.

Ordinary Moments: The Disabled Experience

It's nice when meeting strangers goes that way. Easily. Understandingly. Or so it seemed.

It was time to get dinner started. I continued to talk while crawling around the corner of the room where my wheelchair was parked. As I jumped up and in and began to wheel toward the kitchen, the silent wide-eyed stare of my new friend gave away the words that quickly followed: "Oh, honey, I didn't know you were in a wheelchair."

Apart from the fact that she stretched the word *wheelchair* way beyond its two-syllable limit—she seemed to slide it rather than speak it—this total stranger had called me "honey." The urge to do immediate physical harm was almost overwhelming. No one except my closest friends, my mother, or a lover calls me "honey"—and never ever do they do it to patronize me. ("Honey?" Where the hell is that coming from?)

I wanted to know—needed to know—what difference her subtle observation made. But my talkative friend was now a quiet stranger. She had no answer beyond her obvious unease.

That, in the end, was her answer. She took no time to leave.

The 20 seconds that I took to climb into the chair had abruptly undone the whole half hour before. We weren't going to be friends after all. More than likely, we were never going to see each other again.

And yet she had liked me when I was sitting on the floor. She had liked me before she dripped "honey." She liked my interests, my values, my humor. The only thing she didn't like—couldn't tolerate—was the stereotype she had made of me.

It's her loss. And it's my continuing confusion.

My Body Is New to Me Again

My wheelchair is more than a convenient substitute for my legs. It is, to me, a mode of mental transport as well, an uncommon carrier that has taken me to places I never experienced when I walked. It has caused me pain, and it has caused me pleasure. It has been a source of adventure and the seat of depression. Mostly, though, it has given me a new and different perspective on other people.

When I am in my wheelchair, the world treats me differently. I am pitied and patronized; I was never pitied or patronized when I walked. Now strangers toss loose change in my lap. "God bless you," one says with tearful, serious, sad eyes that never meet mine. Another whispers, "What a shame. She's such a young girl."

My tolerance for the ignorance of others—even well-intentioned others—is tested every day.

There's nothing unusual about learning that your child's developed a slight ear infection. Doctors must tell that to hundreds of mothers a day. No doctor, though, ever told it to any mother the way mine told it to me. He made the usual unusual. And from where I sit, that practice is all too common.

When he looked at me, he saw a 5 year old; in his eyes, I had scant attention span, monosyllabic comprehension, and the responsibility of a Twinkie. He spoke slowly, repetitiously, often singing instead of saying his words. "Do you understand?" he would ask. "Do you understand?" he would ask again. "Let me try to explain it one more time."

I was expecting him to start spelling every word or, perhaps, flash them to me on lotto cards. I feared he might reach across his desk to pat me on the head.

I called him on it. I explained that he need not explain his explanation. He didn't have to go out of his way (all around the mulberry bush, as it were) on my account.

His voice deepened and, as if inspired, began to speak appropriately—like an adult. The silly rhythm disappeared as did the patronizing smiles and nods. He had been trying to be sensitive, he claimed, adding that he felt great sympathy for me.

Sympathy? For me?

I got angry and gave him my speech, the one about all people being individuals, deserving respect and so on. I got angrier and asked him why he'd insulted my intelligence.

He told me I was wasting his time.

Who can say who benefited more from our meeting? Nonetheless, when he sends me his bill for his services, I plan to send him mine for the same.

Not long ago, I overheard one of Ben's classmates tell him that his mother was "ugly cause she can't walk." Without saying a word, Ben tightened and prepared to fight. The two antagonists squared off at the top of the stairs, with me sitting only three stairs below. I crawled up quickly to intervene and to have a quiet necessary talk with them both.

Before I had finished my opening line, the other boy's mother came from nowhere, demanding to know why I was "bothering" her child. She was wearing a particularly obnoxious attitude, but I tried, nonetheless, to explain the circumstances calmly. I indicated that she might find it helpful to review with her son the way in which neither books nor people are judged. As I talked, she tightened, looking a little like Ben had looked only minutes earlier. If this woman had never hated in her life before, I was certain she was hating now. Silently, she led her little victim away.

Over ice cream at home, Ben and I talked about what happened. Ben told me why "that kid was wrong" to have said what he did. "He doesn't even know you," he added. In his own way, Ben was explaining to me what I had tried to explain to the angry mother.

A week later, with Ben's teacher's permission, I visited the classroom to play and to talk with all the kids. I wanted them to get to know and to see Ben's mother as Ben does. After about an hour of easy being-with, it was time for me to leave, and several of the kids—including the one who had only seen me as ugly—walked alongside my chair as I headed to the door. They asked me to come back soon.

Ben was so proud when he returned from school. So was Ben's mother. I wonder, though, when and what I'll hear from that other mother. (Maybe I'll just let Ben handle her.)

The convenience of labels must be for someone else's benefit, certainly not mine.

Recently I phoned a local store manager to inquire about a purchase I had made earlier in the day. In his struggle to recall who I was, he finally asked, "Aren't you the handicapped lady who was in this morning?" That made it so clear and simple for him.

I could only answer, "Which one?"

Being identified by a word you hate is intolerable no matter how common a practice that kind of labeling is. And it's all too common. Absolutely nothing positive is ever associated with any of those labels. How many good things does the word *crippled* bring to mind? *Disabled*? *Handicapped*?

It's too easy for others to consider me very different because a label is applied to me that isn't ever applied to them. That hurts. Words hurt. Because how different am I really? How much more or less am I doing with my life than, say, a "walkie"?

Funny. My friends tell me they hardly ever see the wheelchair anymore. Why is it so strikingly visible to everyone else?

As far as I can tell, someone with a disability is generally assumed either to have lost the capacity for sex or to have given up all interest in it. Speaking for myself, each assumption is demeaning and ridiculous. Yet both persist.

Often I've had the occasion to meet a guy, start dating, and know that an awkwardness over sex is inevitable. (It's a little forward, after all, to announce one's fondness for sex at the first hint of a relationship.) No male yet has simply asked: "Can you have sex?" That's the question, after all. It's right to wonder about it. And it's right to ask it. It's absurd to deny it and worse to disguise it.

There's nothing wrong with a little tact. But let's not forget about straightforwardness. Let's spare us both the unnecessary embarrassment.

In my opinion, sex is one of life's finest pleasures. Nothing I know can replace the experience of intimate sexual contact. That was true before MS. It's just as true now. Maybe even a little more so. Because no one takes a wheelchair to bed.

With the lights dimmed, the chair is easily forgotten. I'm free to be all and only me, one-on-one with another. How could I not love that—and love like that—a lot?

More than a year ago Bob moved in to share his life with Ben and me. He and I travel, we argue, we watch *60 Minutes*, and we get high together. He eats my cooking (a man of courage) and I rub his back. You might say we're an ordinary, happy couple with an ordinary, happy—and sexual— relationship.

This morning, Bob was heading out of town for several days and we were hugging and sharing a good-bye kiss in front of the building. From the gawks on some of the faces passing by, you'd have thought they never saw affection before. I stretched the kiss on purpose hoping to change an attitude or two, but this time not really caring whether I'd succeed.

The City of Boston is my playground, and I've come to know it well. I know its back streets, its front streets, and its alleys. I know, too, that any of these stretches can occasionally mislead even the most seasoned urban wanderer.

Not long ago, I took my weekly trek to the outdoor fruit and vegetable markets in Boston's North End. The sights, sounds, and smells among the crush of people in this lively little part of town never fail to delight, and on this day, they were particularly distracting. I moved, without direction, through it all. Absentmindedly, joyfully, I wandered.

The shrieking horn jolted me back to consciousness—and to the realization that I had become trapped by an unyielding flow of cars. I was, in fact, being forcibly guided up the ramp to the Southeast Expressway, downtown Boston's most formidable speedway. There was no way to turn back against the oncoming blur of traffic. The next exit was 2 or 3 miles ahead.

I started swearing loudly, repeatedly, and determinedly. I was driving with the best of them now, with the legendary Boston drivers. "You dizzy broad!" someone screamed whizzing by. "Go get 'em lady!" another encouraged.

The thundering 18-wheel trucks caused my 4-wheel chair to tremble; every vehicle moved at least 10 times faster than mine. The mid-day heat was softening the tar beneath my tires, and the exhaust from my fellow travelers was making me dizzy. I stared straight ahead, full throttle, praying hard for the next exit.

When the sign finally came into view, it read: "Construction—Take Next Exit." Thank you, God. Thank you, Boston. Thanks a lot!

One-half mile later, my prayers were answered. As I headed down the ramp, calm spilled over me like honey on a cracker. It was time to leave the playground and go home. I would buy my vegetables another day.

From my living room window, the frozen river and the snow-covered buildings look like they'd crack if they were touched. Clumps of overdressed people (stuffed pedestrians) appear to struggle to make slow progress, probably toward a warm shelter nearby. Only a handful of cars creep and slide along the street; the rest are snowed in, broken down, frozen over.

It's cold out there. And I hate it. Wheelchairs weren't made for weather like this.

This morning I took Ben to school, only 3 blocks away. Woman and child against nature—and nature won. Two flat tires, a frozen battery, and icy numbness were the results of my ordeal (sitting in my electric wheelchair, I produce very little protective body heat). Tomorrow Ben will ride with a friend. Tomorrow the repairman will charge me $240.00 to get my chair rolling again. And tomorrow, I still won't be able to go outside.

People tell me I'm smart to stay in, as if the choice were mine, as if I would have no reason to get to work. They point to all the progress I'm able

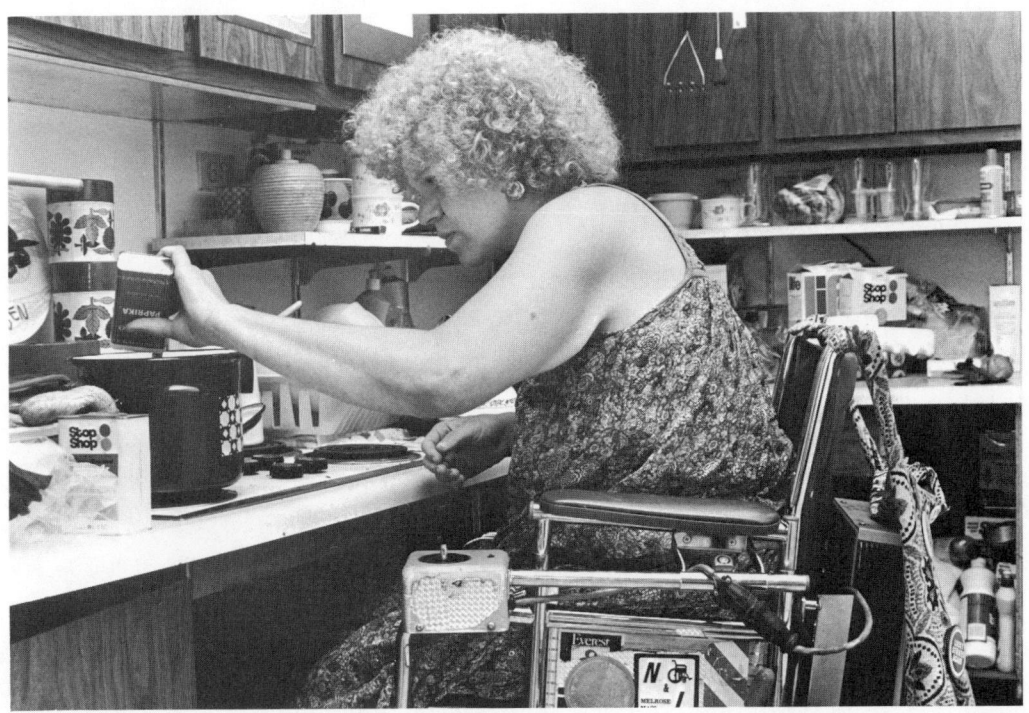

My Body Is New to Me Again

to make in my reading, my painting, and my experimentation in the kitchen. And they even envy my having completed my spring cleaning so early.

To me, though, this unsought gift of spare time makes for an uneasy hibernation. My wheels are already itching for dry pavement.

When I was younger, I studied music extensively and, for awhile, made a slight living playing piano and singing in small clubs. Today, my fingers will not listen to my brain; my playing days, as they say, are over. That's a loss for which I'm not sure I'll ever find an adequate substitute.

I'm aware of so much rhythm in the world: the sun beating down, the tide rushing in, the noises of the city pulsing, driving, ringing, sometimes screaming. It's still important to me to feel the rhythms of life, to experience harmonies in the world around me. I can't stand discord, particularly when its source is other people. If a relationship, for example, should sour, it's as though someone missed a beat (maybe a heartbeat).

I wonder how I affect the harmony of others.

Ben takes music lessons now and enjoys them tremendously. I'm his best listener, his coach, and his critic. He's my newest way to relate to music.

Maybe I want Ben to be the musician I can no longer be. If that's true, I'll never let him know.

I know that many people think my life is so different now with MS. I just don't know why. Why do they choose to believe their misconceptions? Why do they assume the worst and never bother to check their assumptions with me? Does it make them feel better, somehow, to think that I'm worse?

Consider all the abilities a person has. Is walking really such a big deal? Should not walking make such a difference?

Maybe I'm just guilty of being a die-hard optimist. But why not? Doesn't it require just as much effort to be a pessimist? And what fun is that?

In the end, it is attitude that govern one's response to any situation . . . and every situation's response to me.

So until someone makes a law outlawing feeling good, I'll stay an optimist. Afterwards, I'll probably break the law.

Today, a priority in my life is talking with people newly diagnosed as having MS; I remember only too clearly what it felt like to have no one around who understood, who could answer urgent questions, and with whom I could share fears. You should hear the "thank you's" I receive—just for being there and trying to understand.

Sure I'd love for a cure to be found. But I'm not about to mope around just waiting.

I'm often asked what caused my MS. I don't have the answer. Maybe God, with his characteristic good humor, figured, "Debbi, you've been through a lot in your young life. It's time you sat down to take a rest."

Chapter 5

Riding the Iron Worm

Ed Long

Some Definitions

Being handicapped is:

- ◇ When you're the guest of honor at the "Handicapped Person of the Year" award luncheon and the rest room doors are too narrow for the wheelchair. You have to urinate in a broom closet.
- ◇ When someone says to you, "Oh, you have muscular dystrophy? If that happened to me, I'd kill myself."
- ◇ Dropping something, getting a coat hanger, hooking it over what you hope to pick up.
- ◇ Not being able to turn the radio on. Or the television off. Accomplishing microscopic tasks well.
- ◇ Feeling like an emperor—stoned, riding the electric wheelchair down the street (it's like ice skating).
- ◇ Going to the museum and getting in free. (When a non-handicapped person steps back from a work of art, he naturally goes up and down; as I roll back, the artwork recedes and the perspective changes very smoothly.)
- ◇ Seeing everything from about four feet off the ground. (How'd you like to go to a cocktail party when all you can see are rear ends at eye level?)
- ◇ Hating having to ask, all the time ask.
- ◇ Having the ability to sit in one place for 9 hours without going mad from restlessness. (And after 9 hours without moving, to come home and sit in a different chair for 7 more hours.)
- ◇ Feeling violence and anger and having absolutely no strong physical way to express it.

Being handicapped is worrying about being handicapped too much.

But, damn it, this room is a mess, and I can't clean it. I'm hungry, and I can't cook. The window is open and it's freezing outside; I can't shut it. The audiotape is repeating itself over and over, and I can't stop it; the bike's in the way of the player. I hate that tape.

I can't find a pipe that's not clogged, so I can't even get high. And I don't feel like masturbating. Ah, shit!

The incredible pettiness gets wearying at times. I'm always worrying about getting to bed, getting up, getting into a chair, getting out of a chair . . .

Being handicapped creates a pettiness syndrome. All you think about is simple stuff.

Stuff that others never have to consider.

Being handicapped is Rosemary and I spending that weekend together.

I used a sliding board for transfers at the time. Rosemary had polio and wears a brace on her right leg. When the time came for us to go to bed, I showed Rosemary how to remove the arm from the wheelchair so I could slide the board under me. Then she sat on the bed in order to pull me over to her. That's how it's supposed to work.

Rosemary wasn't quite strong enough to get me across in one pull, and when she tugged I pitched over sideways. My head was on the bed, my ass was in the wheelchair, and my side and shoulder just barely balanced on the board. She tried pulling me by the arm, but I almost fell completely over. She raised herself higher on the bed and pulled harder. The situation was becoming ridiculous. If I fell on the floor, she would never get me up again. If she fell, she'd have a tough time getting up. We both laughed hysterically, uncontrollably, at our predicament.

Finally, with a mighty burst, I rolled over, Rosemary yanked on my belt, and there I was: in bed.

Our laughing continued. And our lovemaking began.

For every 6 months, from birth until age 14, I went to the hospital to demonstrate my "condition." Never did I see the same doctor twice. Never did any kind of treatment or prescription or advice come my way.

No physical therapy.

No occupational therapy.

No psychological therapy.

No counseling of any kind.

I never knew anything about muscular dystrophy until I was in my early 30's.

Yardsticks

My brother Bob, 3 years younger than I, was always an accurate yardstick against which to measure dystrophy's progress.

When I was 8, I won all of our fights. When I was 10, he won about 25 percent. When I turned 12, he went over the 50 percent mark. And by the time I was 14, he won them all.

So I started throwing things at him. Eventually, I only cursed.

Then, of course, there was the standard provided by stairs. How hard were they to climb? How fast could I run down them? How did I look while doing either? And who might be watching?

These were the questions I asked between 5 and 14. Then, increasingly, I added another: Who would help me up if I fell down?

Falling. It was always on my mind.

Falling. It was the fear that got to me the most.

Every single day of my life I have worried about:

⋄ My ankles giving way or bending out.

⋄ My foot dropping and pointing downward.

⋄ My calves tightening.

⋄ My heel cords shortening.

Falling. Going upstairs and falling.
Going downstairs and falling.
Answering the call of nature and falling.

When I was younger and I walked, I fought stairs. Now, from my wheelchair, I continue the same battle.

They'll probably have my funeral in an inaccessible funeral parlor—after Mass in an inaccessible church.

Anne and Freddie were lying on an old bedspring. I was 10 years old at the time. And I was jealous.

Freddie and I began to fight for Anne's attention, and, almost immediately, she spoke up for me. I began to puff with pride.

"Leave him alone, Freddie. He's crippled."

Falling for Mary

Walking across the grass at Carson Beach with Freddie and Bill. There's the beautiful and desirable Mary sitting on a blanket, alone. We were all 14 and cocky.

We swagger toward Mary and just as we approach the blanket's fringe, *I fall down*.

Falling. Always falling. Always at the worst times.

In those days, I walked up on my toes, and every now and then my knees would buckle. I'd fall straight down with my behind often landing painfully on the heel of my shoe as my leg bent under me.

I stretched out my leg, and Fred put his heel against my foot for support. I got up in stages, laboriously, pushing my hands first against my calves, then against my knees, and finally against my thighs.

I blushed in an agony of shame for at least 10 minutes.

It's Routine

To know that I was getting worse month by month. To me this seemed the most natural thing in the world.

I remember getting up from my bed at age 17.

Up on my right elbow, then up on my left. A pull with my body to the left, and I would straighten my right arm. Then a pull to the right, and I'd straighten my left. Then I'd swing my legs over the side of the bed.

What a joy to spring out of bed when I was 10! Quickly pull on a t-shirt and chinos, yank on the socks and sneakers and go. Total time from up to out: roughly 2 minutes.

No springing by 20. I would reach out and pull on my pants. Then, by putting one leg on the bed and bending my foot sideways, I'd be able to slide on my socks and shoes. Then I'd lean to the right, push with my arms, lean my head against the wall, put my knees against the edge of the bed, balance, turn, hold the metal chair, then grab the desk, take four or five steps to the bureau, hold on, then walk down the hallway to the bathroom, then the kitchen, then out. Total time: about 35 minutes.

By the time I was 20, my routine of 10 years earlier took more than half an hour longer.

I guess I began having trouble with the routine around 19 or so. I'd have to have Dad undress me. I remember him kneeling down to help pull off my pants (I think I was able to take off my shirt by myself; I'm not sure).

Dad put a buzzer by my head on the bed and wired it to sound in his room. When I pushed, the buzzer would let him know I needed help. Bob would help me sometimes, and, sometimes, Mother.

I remember Dad falling asleep in his chair after Mother had gone to bed. I remember trying to wake him up to help me to bed. I started with calling. Then yelling. I remember finally throwing paperback books at him until he responded.

I've spent a lot of time trying to wake people up.

It's very hard for me to cough. When I had pneumonia in 1968, and again in 1974, coughing was the biggest problem. I'd cough all night long just to do the work of one good, normal, strong cough.

With muscular dystrophy, I don't suffer any pain, or any lack of pain.

If I close my eyes I don't feel like I have MD. Then I try to do something, and I see again—that I can't. The will to move is there; the simple strength is not.

Progress

In 1973, the doctors told me I didn't have Duchenne's muscular dystrophy anymore. I had lived too long, they said. I must have limb-girdle dystrophy instead.

In 1977, they said it wasn't limb-girdle after all; I was too healthy for limb-girdle. I must have Becker's; they said, a milder form of dystrophy.

The next time I go, maybe they'll tell me I'm completely cured!

Riding the Iron Worm

I was sitting on the corner of 170th and Broadway, just watching the crowd go by. Dominicans, Italians, Puerto Ricans, Greeks—all the minorities of the city of New York. It was one of those steamy summer days, but I was feeling pretty good being out in the world.

A man wheeling himself in a beaten-up old chair came around the corner. "Hey, brother, how's it going?" I asked. He looked surprised to see someone else in a chair.

"Good. You?"

We sat and talked easily. David had a beard, black hair, thin legs, well-muscled arms, and broad shoulders. He had cerebral palsy, he explained, and had lived on Fort Washington Avenue all his life. He was 27.

After about a half hour, he looked at his watch and said, "Well, I gotta move on."

"Where are you headed?" I asked.

"Gotta get down to 42nd Street."

"Calling a taxi?"

"Hell, no. I'm going by subway."

"Subway?" I was amazed. "How do you do that?"

"Follow me. You'll find out." He began to wheel, and I followed in my electric.

When we arrived at the entrance to the 168th Street subway, directly in front of Columbia Presbyterian Hospital, I was transfixed by the long, steep stairway. "You're going down there?" I asked. I was doubtful.

"Sure. Gotta get the right person, though." David sat, closely examining each passerby.

Before too long, a man looking to be about 60 stopped to ask whether David needed help. "No. No thanks," David answered and then knowingly adviced me, "He's too old."

Two nurses soon followed. "Can we help you?"

"No. I'm fine thanks," he smiled, and, as we both watched them head down he added, "not quite strong enough."

He allowed about 15 more people to go by and then announced, "Here comes my man now. Watch this." A dark complexioned man, early 20s, and about 5'8" was striding toward us. When he got close enough, David asked, "Think you might help me down these stairs?"

"Sure. Fine. What do I do?"

"Great. Just grab the handles, put your foot on that pipe near the ground, and tilt me back." With little hesitation, the man followed David's instructions. David grabbed the railing with his left hand and held the wheel rim with his right. The man began easing the chair down one step at a time.

"See you later, Ed," he called up. "Nice meeting you." I watched him make it down the long flight and wondered where he found the courage.

I met and talked again with David several times over the next couple of weeks and grew more impressed with him at every meeting. He was, I learned, a photographer and traveled to 42nd Street 3 or 4 times every week to take pictures of tourists. He'd shoot in Times Square sometimes until 3:00 or 4:00 a.m., and often he'd wind up stuck in the subway for hours waiting for the right person to come along and help him up the stairs.

I thought about David a lot. And I thought about the subway. The last time I had ridden it, I was 14 years old. That was 20 years ago. I knew I was now deciding it was time to ride again.

"We should definitely try it one of these days," Alice answered immediately when I finally mentioned the challenge to her. Alice, my girlfriend for several years, is about 5'3" with a slight but solid build. She had short, strong legs and seemed to have inherited a wiry toughness from her Russian forebears. "If you use the manual chair and I take the front and we find some big guy to hang onto the back—I'm sure it'll work."

I started hanging around the subway entrance several times a week, just checking things out. Maybe Alice was a little more certain than I about our chances.

"Hey, Alice, let's have dinner tonight in the Village." After 3 weeks, I had made up my mind. Going to the Village meant taking the subway. And I was already terrified. My stomach was jumping, my hands sweating. I felt a cold wetness along my sides as we headed out.

I looked carefully, as David had, at the people passing the entrance to the subway. "Nope. He's too thin. Don't like his looks. Nope, they don't look quite right either." My careful scrutiny excluded the first 30 or so candidates; I even let slip a few who were probably solid prospects. But I was getting ready. "Well, Alice, we can't stay here all day."

A man, about 30, came along. He looked Greek, good build, a little on the short side. "Would you mind giving us a hand, sir?"

"Sure. Tell me what to do."

I explained very carefully. "Grab the handles. Tilt the chair back onto the big wheels. She'll take the front."

Alice moved into position and, by holding the footrests, helped to keep the chair tilted back. I was feeling confident, sort of. The man seemed sure of himself, and the chair felt balanced.

Down we went, one step at a time. Slowly. And then we reached the first landing. "You okay, Alice?"

"No problem."

"And how are you doing back there?"

"Very good."

"Okay," I said, "next flight."

Finally, we hit bottom. "Hey, thanks a lot."

"No problem." And the man walked off, leaving Alice and me smiling back and forth at each other triumphantly.

The train arrived within minutes, and Alice pushed the chair in and locked the brakes. The doors closed, and we were off.

What a feeling! First time on the subway in 20 years! Impossible to describe.

After 15 minutes of riding, I began to worry again. How would we get up the stairs at the other end? What if nobody was around to help?

Sixteenth Street, our stop. We left the train and merged with the huge crowd heading for the stairs. "Here, let us give you a hand." A big burly guy was offering himself and his even burlier friend. My worrying was over. Two more strangers lent themselves silently to the task as well. The four carried the chair and me, smoothly and without any apparent effort, up the long flight. The wheels never touched the stairs. What secure joy. No way they would have dropped me. And they didn't.

"All right. Thanks a lot. Really!"

There we were—Alice and I—in Greenwich Village. A whole new world to explore. I had done it. We had done it. Me. Alice. Some total but willing strangers. And, of course, David. Thank you, David.

The evening couldn't have been better. Dinner. Wandering. Watching. Laughing. A perfect and delightful night. And when the time came to return uptown, two strong strangers appeared in moments and helped me down to the train. The easiest of endings.

Alice and I were the only two passengers to emerge from the train at the 168th Street Station; it was totally deserted. Because of the hour, we knew that trains would be slow in coming, but we waited nonetheless in contented quiet. We were confident now that there was no cause to worry. Help would be riding on the next train.

Twenty minutes later, an old man, three drunks, and a mother dragging a crying baby proved us wrong. So we waited some more.

The station showed no signs of life. Stone silence. Finally Alice said quietly, "I want to try it. I think we can do it."

"I don't know, Alice. It won't be easy."

We continued to wait.

"Come on Ed, I can do it."

"Okay. Let's go."

Alice moved behind me, tilted the chair backwards, and pulled me up one step. "How's it feel?" I asked, concerned.

"Good." Up another step. I was growing increasingly nervous. Four steps. Six steps. Alice was into a rhythm: heave and rest, heave and rest. By the tenth step, I could hear that she was weakening. Her breathing was quick and harsh. And we were only about halfway up.

She stopped. "I can't do anymore. Ed. I just can't."

There we were, balancing on a step somewhere in the middle of the longest flight of stairs I'd ever seen. Sweating and gasping, Alice hung onto the handles, keeping the chair tilted back. I was gripping the armrests tightly, my knuckles white with strain. The chair began to sway precariously. I was beginning to envision the inevitable.

"Help!" she cried weakly.

"Help! Help!" I screamed loudly.

The station stayed silent. We were alone.

"Help! Help!" In unison now.

Then, at the bottom of the stairs, a welcome sight. A guard. "That you screaming like that?" he wanted to know. "What's going on?"

"Can you help us please?" I asked. "She can't hold the chair here much longer."

"You know," he said as he took his time up the stairs, "you aren't supposed to be down here in no wheelchair." I thought it best not to enter into a debate just now.

The guard grabbed the footrests and pushed hard. The force knocked Alice down to a sitting position from which she clung desperately to the handles. "No," I yelled, "don't push!"

"Well, then, what the hell do you want me to do?" He was clearly annoyed.

"Could you just please get in the back of the chair?" I asked with all the calmness I could muster.

"No," Alice interrupted. "If he let's go now, we'll fall."

We were stuck. Muttering angrily, the guard let go with one hand and reached for his intercom. "This is Area 267. I need assistance. Need assistance." He was sounding very official, very in charge. No one answered him. Despite his repeated calls for "assistance," all we could hear was static.

"I'll do it," said Alice. There was grit in her voice. "I've got to do it." She stooped up and heaved. We all moved up one step.

"You just keep holding on, okay?" I asked the guard.

"Yeah, I'll hold on. You know, you're not supposed to be here, don't you. This wouldn't be happening if you weren't here, like you're supposed to not be here."

Alice jerked the chair up another step and rested. Up still another and rested again. Two more. Four more. And then, there we were. Out. We had made it.

Alice sat down where she was and started to cry uncontrollably. I breathed deeply and thanked God.

"Remember what I'm telling you," the guard barked. "You don't belong down here. I don't never want to see you down here again."

"Will you go away and leave us alone," Alice cried wearily. It was more of a command than a request. "And thanks for your help."

"Just keep out of here," he mumbled and walked away.

Alice and I both sat for a long quiet time, just looking at each other.
"I don't know how I did that, Ed. Honestly I don't."
"You did it because you had to. You didn't have a choice."
We held each other.
We knew we had beaten the rattler. We had ridden the iron worm.

Gloria

The phone rang at 8:00 a.m. Alice, busying herself to leave for school, answered it in a rush. It was Gloria, the attendant who got me up every morning.

"Alice, I just remembered I have to go to Housing Court today. Can you get Ed up for me?"

"Well, I guess I'll have to, even though I'm going to be late," Alice answered. "Please try to give us a little more notice from now on, alright?"

"Yeah. Right. Sorry. It won't happen again. Promise."

One week later, just about 8:00 a.m., the phone rang. "Alice. It's Gloria. I'm really sorry, but I just remembered I have to go to court again."

"Please, Gloria, let us know ahead of time. Don't let this happen again, okay? See you tomorrow." Alice was less than thrilled.

The next day, everyone left the house a little before 8:00 a.m. At 8:30, when Gloria was expected, the phone rang. And rang. I awakened with a start, and that old nervous, jumpy-stomach feeling clicked in. Shit! That's Gloria, and I'll bet she's not coming.

The ringing stopped. Maybe it wasn't her. Maybe someone else was calling. I waited. Then the phone rang three times and stopped; that was Gloria's signal letting me know she was on her way.

I went back to sleep until the phone again jolted me awake. I knew it was Gloria. I was stuck. Absolutely helpless. I closed my eyes and tried going back to sleep. No use. My mind kind of drifted.

I was now completely awake—alone and afraid. My feet and hands were wet with sweat, my stomach was quivering. Gloria was not coming. Alice would be at school all day and was visiting her mother that night. I wouldn't see her again until 9:00 or 10:00 p.m. Beth wouldn't be home until then either. Nan had stayed at a friend's house, and I had no idea when she'd be home. I wasn't expecting visitors.

The shaking and nervousness began to spread from my stomach up into my chest. I had the feeling that when it reached my head I'd crack up.

By now I had urinated several times and the urinal was completely filled. But I had to go again. I dumped some of the urine out onto the floor. (Once, in my previous apartment I had to do the same thing and wound up pouring the urine into my shoes.)

I began shouting for help. I could hear the woman upstairs walking around. Why wasn't she hearing me? I yelled for awhile and then rested. Yelled and rested. I knew she was Spanish and racked my brains for words to use in case she showed up. How do you say "put on my shirt and pants" in Spanish? How do you say "call the cops"?

I tried hard to stop panicking, took deep breaths, concentrated on being calm. My claustrophobic fear diminished. I was getting a little calmer. I was reaching a quieter plateau.

Roughly 3 hours passed. The phone rang four different times. No one showed up.

How strange it was to hear tiny noises upstairs and conversations in the street and yet, no matter how loudly I screamed, no one could hear me. It was as though I were in some kind of vacuum.

I could also hear the elevator door crashing shut and other apartment doors on my floor opening and closing. Still no one could hear me.

More time crawled by, hours measured in minutes. Then, finally, noises from the front door. "Hey! Hello! Who is it? In here!"

Nan appeared in the doorway.

"Oh, no!" she cried. "All this time and Gloria never came!"

I was depressed for the rest of the day—what remained of it. I had been brought face to face with my own helplessness, my utter dependence.

A few days later, Gloria called. She said she thought we had gone to Boston when the phone rang so often without anyone answering.

I told her not to come back anymore.

I could never trust her again.

Alone

Who would imagine a pain-filled, life-and-death struggle taking place around an armchair and a footstool? Who would believe that a deep spiritual experience could take place between 8:30 and 10:00 p.m. on an otherwise uneventful Tuesday? While watching television, yet.

It all began when Peter, Alice, Kathy, Michael, and Ana went out. I was alone in the house, comfortably seated in an armchair, enjoying the rare calm. "Mystery Movie" was playing on the tube, with Helen Hayes starring in *The Snoop Sisters*. I'd seen the picture before and hated it. But because the set was out of my reach, I couldn't turn the channel.

A soft breeze blew a 5-dollar bill off the window sill and onto the floor. I automatically leaned forward to pick it up. Now this is *not* one of my moves, and I quickly found myself pitched forward with both feet on the ground, my head between my knees, one arm stretched out for the 5 and the other resting on the foot stool directly in front of me. There was no way I was going to get up from that position!

In short order, my legs began to ache at the hip joints and the knees. Working my right leg forward just a bit, I only caused the pain to grow sharper. Clever. With my head and one arm now resting on the stool in an effort to take some pressure off the legs, I knew I had done it: one of my "situations" again. What now?

It was 8:30 at night. Peter would be the first one home, but not before 11:00. I couldn't possibly remain in this position for the next 2½ hours.

Can you picture this? One knee was on the floor. The other leg was bent almost double, with that knee just about touching my chin. Not real comfortable.

I grabbed the edge of the stool and tried to pull myself up. No good. Then I tried to push the stool out of the way. No good again. Then I figured if I pulled the stool with my teeth and pushed hard with my hand . . . that didn't work either.

The pain was terrible and mounting. I began to tear at the stool with my teeth. I was drenched with sweat!

"Help! Somebody! Please help! Michael! Anna! Alice! Anybody! Help! Help me!" I screamed non-stop to no avail. And every time I tried to maneuver myself into a better position, my strategy backfired. The situation was going from bad to bleak. I knew my legs wouldn't last until 11:00.

"Please, God! Get me out of this! Get me out and I'll go back to church! I promise! Please! Jesus, Please!" I was panicking wildly.

The phone rang. *The phone.* I hadn't thought of the phone. Damn. I'll call somebody!

In order to reach the phone on the table where it sat, I'd have to lean back on one leg and push against the table with my head. This meant I had to decide which leg I wanted to break. If I leaned anymore on either one, it was certain to snap. Of this I was certain. But what choice did I have? So I made my move. It would be the right leg.

Horrible pain burst from the right hip joint as I leaned back. But I kept pushing at the table. My glasses slid down and off my face. I pushed some more and succeeded in knocking the receiver off the hook. Score one for persistence.

Now to dial "O" for operator. But I quickly discovered I didn't have enough strength to get the damn dial all the way around. (Why hadn't I thought of dialing 411? It would have been so much easier.) I kept at it, over and over, meeting with increasingly less success. My pain was fast becoming unbearable.

"Son of a bitch! Bastard! Mother f . . ." The rotary dial made it to the halfway point. "I'm going to dial this fucking, sucking phone if it's the last goddamn thing . . ." Then all the way around. I did it!

"Operator," I yelled. The mouthpiece was at least 2 feet away. "Operator! Call the fire department!" The station was just at the end of my street; they could be here in no time. "I'm crippled! I'm in trouble! Get help!"

A man's voice came on the line, faintly. "Fire department."

"Send help! I'm handicapped. I'm on the floor. Hurry!"

"What's the address?"

"139 Concord. Please hurry! Please help!"

"What's your name?"

"My name? Never mind! My leg is breaking. Do you understand that? My leg is breaking. I'm on the floor . . ."

"What floor you on?"

"The first. The first floor. Christ! Please! Get here right away."

"All right. All right now. Just hang in there."

The line went dead. I screamed in agony and followed up with a prolonged groan.

I couldn't be sure how much time passed when I heard the sirens. Two engines and a ladder truck pulled up to my house. Flashing lights. Loud voices. I was on the edge of blacking out. "Here I am! I'm in here! Help me! Quick!"

Five firemen burst in, fully decked in their metal headgear, heavy raincoats, and boots. They carried an assortment of axes and hooks.

"There he is," someone yelled. "Pick him up."

Two men rushed over and tried to lift me out of position. My behind caught on the seat cushion, and it went up with me. "My legs," I groaned. "My legs."

Two other men came around behind the chair. One knocked over a lamp just as the other tripped over the stereo cord. Everything came crashing down noisily. Together, the four firemen carried me gently back into the chair. I felt as if I had just been blessed. What relief!

The firemen picked up the stereo and the lamp and retrieved my glasses. "I'm all right now. Thanks. Thanks a lot."

"Let us call an ambulance for you."

"No. No need. That's all right. I'm fine now." I could tell that nothing, in fact, was broken. There really was no need for a hospital. Nonetheless, the men milled around a little while longer until they were sure I was okay.

As soon as they left, I began to shake with cold and nerves. My hands were flying around on their own. I felt sick and leaned back to try to capture some deep breaths.

Crash! The front door again! Two guys I hadn't seen before rushed in with a stretcher. "City Hospital. You called for an ambulance?"

"No." I was stunned. "Not me." I was afraid they'd take me to the hospital anyway. "I'm fine. Don't need an ambulance at all. Really."

"Well, okay then. If you're sure about that." And the two strangers left.

A fireman quickly returned. "Forgot to take this hook here." He smiled and, more importantly, he left.

The Snoop Sisters were still chatting on about something. Helen Hayes was tiptoeing through an old, dark warehouse. I could have sworn I'd been on the floor for at least 3 hours and yet it wasn't even 10:00.

Thank you, God. Thanks for making that phone ring.

A knock on the door, a soft one. "Come in."

In walked Peaches, a beautiful prostitute, a friend of a friend. "Heard you might want to see a woman tonight," she purred. "All I need is 10 bucks."

Now I've been a Peaches fan for awhile and had been desiring her for at least a month; I'd put word out. But why (oh why) did she have to show up now? Tonight. Of all nights.

"Listen, Peaches. I'm sorry. I couldn't do a thing tonight. I'm too tired even to get out of this chair. I'm really sorry."

"Okay. I understand. No problem. Maybe later."

We talked for a brief while, and she left me to myself. I resumed my shaking, my sweating, and my feeling sick. I tried, unsuccessfully, to rest.

When Peter returned, I had him lift me right to bed.

For the next 2 weeks, I was in aching agony. I talked about nothing else but that night to everyone. My spiritual experience. My talks with God . . . and with the operator.

Kids

I'm not afraid of anybody or anything. I used to hang out in Needle Park a lot, on Broadway and 72nd. No one ever bothered me. The cops knew I wasn't an addict. The addicts knew I wasn't a cop. And everyone knew I was as poor as they were.

Central Park at night. Harlem and 128th. I've lived in the South End for 4 years. I'm never afraid on the street. Well, hardly ever.

I had driven my electric wheelchair into the playground and was having an aimless good time just riding around. A couple of kids approached. They looked to be about 8 or 9 years old. "Hi, Mister. How's that work?"

"Runs on a battery," I answered.

"How do you steer it?"

"Like this," I said and moved the control slightly.

They stared, fascinated.

I was smiling, feeling good, talking to these interested kids. Honest curiosity is always refreshing.

The pair stepped back a couple of paces. Suddenly I got a chill and felt a gray feeling. I eyed them closely. One leaned close to the other, and I could hear a low voice, the beginning of a plan: "You push him out; I'll grab the chair."

A scared helpless feeling crawled over me. These kids weren't out to hit me or rob me. They weren't hating me for the color of my skin; they were white like me. They just figured my chair would be a terrific toy. They'd take off on their little joy ride, and I'd be stuck lying on the ground. It wasn't cruelty on their part. It was simply their total uninvolvement with me as a person. Maybe that was cruelty of a different sort.

I shoved the control forward and headed out of the park. If only I could make it to Columbus Avenue where there'd be lots of people around. If I could just keep ahead of them.

"Hey, Mister. Come back. There's a nice hill over here for you to ride down."

There was more threat in those high tinny voices than what you'd hear from twice as many muggers. Nice hill, my ass.

I reached Columbus, safely. As a couple of strangers approached, the little punks stopped their chase and backed away.

Later that same day I rode on a South End tour, and in about 2 hours I found myself on that same street again. I fled. That's the only way to describe it. I got off that street so fast.

To this day, I won't go on it.

Looking Back

I was part of a large gathering attending a muscular dystrophy seminar: speakers, panels, films—the works. Practically everyone there had muscular dystrophy.

After one of the panels, Alice, Willy and his girl, and I went for a drink. Willy has MD. He's about 21 and looks to me as if he has about a year before he'll have to go into a wheelchair.

When we had finished our drink and it was time to go, Willy pushed back from the table. His girl got up and stood by his chair. He stuck out his leg.

I began to have a strange flashback. He was making every single move I used to make when I was at his stage of MD.

She put her foot behind his to keep him from slipping. Willy pushed down on the table, raised himself halfway up, and began to strain. He was right at the crucial time when the left leg might give way (and down you go again). His face reddened, and he began to sweat. Push. Push. Finally, with a great heave, he was up. A triumphant smile covered his face celebrating his victory, his conquering of enormous physical odds.

I was about to say "Hey, I used to get up the same way!" But I thought better of it.

I used to think I was the only person who suffered and overcame the way I did. Each one of my small victories, I believed, was uniquely and intensely my own. I thought with pride that my struggle had never been shared by anyone else.

My smile used to be the same as Willy's.

So I said nothing as Willy flaunted his pride around the table. "That's the kind of struggle I go through. I'm tougher than anybody here."

His look. So clear and so familiar to me. So much a part of my life.

Willy was a window into my past.

Soon to be his past as well.

Marie

Marie was a comfortable, secure harbor after the misery and storm of Cheryl. She had a calming effect on me. Tall, smiling, large-mouthed black woman with a wonderful figure. A regular ego balm, Marie.

We met first at the Employment Center and then, a couple of months later, at a party. "Dance with me?" she asked, smiling. It was an invitation. I accepted at once.

Marie wheeled my chair onto the dance floor and wrapped her arms gently around me. I was enveloped in a warm, perfumed darkness, my head against her breasts, my arms around her legs.

A beautiful feeling. The first time I'd been touched by a woman in 4 years.

After the dance she sat on one of the stereo speakers, I sat in front of her, and we kissed. And kept on kissing. I was leaning so far forward that I almost fell out of the chair. But I couldn't stop holding her. We didn't talk much. We didn't need to.

A week later, we went out to dinner. In the car heading home, she looked so sensual, and her thigh felt so good next to me. I was getting very excited, and she could tell.

"Don't rush things," she said. "All in good time."

That remark sent me flying. "All in good time." We held hands and kissed good night.

We had an even more splendid date the next week. Marie cooked a delicious meal at my apartment. Good wine and a fresh bottle of Chivas. Candles. Romantic music. An after-dinner joint. She sat in my armchair; I sat in my wheelchair in front of her. Warm, passionate embraces.

We were alone and, of course, this meant there was no way for me to be lifted into bed. So, instead, we embraced and kissed in this position for hours. This kind of situation, a pleasant frustration (with the emphasis on frustration), continued on several more occasions. Until finally . . .

It was a cold January night. Marie came over after Russ had gone out with his girlfriend, Joyce. The evening took its usual course. At about 2:00 a.m., the apartment was getting noticeably warmer. "Would you mind if I took my girdle off?"

"Mind? No. Not at all."

"Of course you wouldn't mind," she laughed.

When she came out of the bathroom, she sat in the chair and stretched out her legs. She had removed her stockings. Her skirt was up around her waist. Her legs were smooth. Her thighs were large and strong. We were both aroused.

Russ and Joyce came home about an hour later and went directly into the kitchen. By now, I had been in the wheelchair all day and all night, and I was very sore and tired. I looked over at the couch.

"Hey, Russ. Give me a lift, will you?" Russ came in and lifted me onto the couch. Marie sat beside me.

Suddenly it hit me: Here I was sitting next to Marie *on the couch*! (Translation: We could have sex!)

Russ and Joyce left, and soon Marie and I were lying side by side. After a short while, she sat up and took off her blouse and her bra.

"Can I kiss your breasts?" I asked.

"I'd like that very much," she replied.

"Marie, let's do it."

"No, Ed. I mean I have to be comfortable first." And then she asked me, "How long since you've had sex?"

"I've never had it."

"Never? Are you serious?" She looked at me, surprised. "How did you manage this long without going crazy?"

"I had no choice, that's all. I had to manage."

She kissed me compassionately. "I'm coming over tomorrow night, and we're going to do it."

"Will you? Really? That'll be good. Please do that."

She ran her hands softly all over my body. It was 6:00 a.m. and beginning to get light when Marie left.

All the next day I was a nervous wreck. What would happen? What if I couldn't do anything? Maybe she'd change her mind. I worried non-stop.

"Russ, when I let you know, you'll help me into bed, okay? And then you'll go out, right?"

The night finally arrived. Russ, Marie, and I sat around and talked. I was nervous and miserable. By midnight I realized I had to do something.

"Russ, help me into the bathroom, will you?"

He wheeled me in. All right, Ed, I told myself firmly, you've been fooling around long enough. It's now or never. Go to it!

"Russ, push me into the bedroom. Quick. Now get me onto the bed."

"Ed," Marie called. "Where are you, Ed?"

Russ put out the bedroom light and left. I kept silent, quivering under the sheet. And I waited. Would she come in? What would she say? What would I do?

I heard Russ go out the front door. A Nancy Wilson record was playing softly. The house was still and quiet. Then I heard Marie lock the front door.

She appeared at the bedroom door, smiling. "How you doing. Ed?"

"Oh," in a shaking voice, "I'm good." My stomach was churning; I was hoping she wouldn't hear it.

Without making a sound, Marie walked slowly to the window and undressed. The street light peeked through the blinds making stripes on her beautiful body. Her breasts seemed to leap out at me. She kept her panties on.

Then I felt her lying next to me. "Relax," she whispered. "I'm just going to sleep for awhile." She closed her eyes and lay still.

Soon, we began to kiss, and I put my arm around her. She took off her panties and kicked them to the foot of the bed. Then she put her leg over me, stroking and caressing. I was hard.

"How are we going to do this?" she asked.

"How about me getting on top?" I suggested. We pushed and pulled, and finally, I was where I wanted to be. But by this time, tired and sweating, I was hardly ready to perform.

"Well, nothing's going to happen this way," she said.

"No. I guess not. Let's try it with you on top."

She looked surprised. "You sure I won't hurt you?"

"You won't. I'm sure. Go ahead."

She reversed positions and, now on top, started moving her body all around me. With little effect. "This is too frustrating," she said. "I can't do anything with you. You understand, don't you? It's just that it's making me so nervous."

"Yeah, Marie. I guess I understand."

She moved off to lie beside me. "How do you feel?" she asked.

Riding the Iron Worm

"Well . . . frustrated, I guess. And disappointed. Will you come back tomorrow night?"

"I'll try, Ed. You do understand, don't you?" she repeated.

"Don't worry about it." Then Marie stood up, dressed, and left.

Russ came home a little while later. "Ed, you stud you. How'd you make out? How're you feeling?"

He was so enthusiastic. I didn't have the heart to answer him.

Two days later, Marie returned. We went through the same preliminaries. Russ helped me to bed and disappeared. Marie undressed and lay alongside me. We kissed and felt each other.

"We can't do anything," she said suddenly, "because I'm having my period."

I was disappointed. And I was relieved.

I caressed her. Her body writhed and twisted. Spasms began to shake her. When she eventually lay still, we continued to kiss and hold each other. Then she left.

A week went by, and I heard nothing from Marie. A long week. I tried calling her, but each time I reached her she explained one reason or another why she couldn't come by. Finally, after repeated phone calls, she agreed to see me again.

I was already in bed when she walked into the room. This time, she pulled a chair over. I urged her to come into bed with me. When she did, she stayed fully dressed. We kissed and talked, and, after a couple of hours, Marie went home.

It was over.

Here's Looking At You

Some people never look at a handicapped person. To them, I'm the Invisible Man.

Others sneak looks. When I catch their eyes, they quickly look away.

When I changed to an electric wheelchair, people's looks went from pitying to admiring. There were noticeably more smiles, as well, and these were frequently accompanied by questions: How does that work? How fast does it go? How much does it cost?

Recently, I went to a neighborhood fair and sat in the middle of at least 1000 people. No one looked at me. No one.

I freaked out.

Unhappy when they look, unhappy when they don't.

Chapter 6

I Would Be This Way Forever

Meg Kocher

In the 1940s, people were terrified of polio. Almost daily, newspapers tallied the "sufferers of the dreaded ailment," as the then highly contagious virus reached epidemic proportions. I was 3 when it got me.

One day I was running and playing as usual; the next I was listless, fussy, grouchy. My temperature soared. My legs and my back stiffened and hurt. My parents reacted with horror, guilt, and compassion to the unmistakable diagnosis.

I was taken to a hospital in Fort Wayne, Indiana, the nearest large city, where I stayed for 12 days. When I returned home, my father went door-to-door in our town of 8000 to find a nurse to come and take care of me. It took him awhile to find someone.

People were so afraid of polio. In the grocery store, parents hid their children behind their backs when they saw my mother approach. My sisters were whisked away to our grandparents' house "for safety."

Finally, though, a retired nurse, dubbed Aunt Mary, agreed to move in. She stayed with us for 9 months.

Aunt Mary did exercises with me and regularly applied heated compresses—hot packs—to my legs. My back and right leg responded to her treatment, gaining strength, but my left leg remained weak. Within 2 months, I began walking with crutches and with a brace on my left leg. Several months later, I began to ride my tricycle again. Aunt Mary promised to buy me an ice cream cone if I rode my tricycle uptown.

After Aunt Mary left, my sisters continued to help me. When we played and I got tired, they pulled me around in the wagon. I learned to ride a two-wheel bike, to climb trees, and to swim. With time, in fact, and with some adaptations, I learned to do most things.

All this time, though, my parents never talked to me about polio; how it had affected me or what would happen to me in the future. They were denying that I was different from my sisters, assuming instead that if they treated me like them, everything would work out fine. I didn't want special treatment, but I did need to understand my differentness.

I was learning that being disabled was a bad thing to be. I felt I caused my parents' guilt ("How could we have prevented that?"), my friends' discomfort ("Should we invite her or shouldn't we?"), and the awkwardness and patronizing manner of others around me ("Well, aren't *we* doing better today."). Although my disability was moderate, the negative messages affected me deeply. My disability was no longer just a part of me—my legs; it was all of me. I was convinced that I was a bad, stupid, worthless, ugly person and that I could do nothing to change this. I would be this way forever.

I have spent much of my life struggling to resolve these feelings, to integrate the physical me with all the rest of me. This was the challenge that my disability presented, the challenge that took me 25 years to overcome. Until I succeeded, my skinny legs ran my life.

Twenty-five years later, I have emerged as a fighter, working to build an interdependent community of disabled peers that's based on pride and compassion. What follows chronicles the important parts of that emergence.

No one else in our town used a brace and crutches. No one used a wheelchair, a guide dog, or an interpreter. There was only the man who walked funny, the man people called stupid and dumb. And there was the girl, 1 year younger than I, who had polio but who didn't need a brace or crutches. These were my peers, my models of what it meant to be disabled. I felt very different, very weird.

I was interpreting polio as a punishment. Every night I asked God what I had done as a 3 year old that deserved such horrible treatment. Also, I looked to the future as a kind of salvation; I knew that none of the high school kids used braces or used crutches, so I assumed that when I got older I wouldn't need mine either. I never figured out the details; I just figured I'd grow out of them somehow.

In seventh grade, my feelings of differentness became acute. Like most adolescents, I was extremely self-conscious of my body. In particular, I noticed how the other girls' lower legs were filling out, becoming shapely. I waited for that to happen to mine; no one had prepared me for the fact that they would remain skinny. One teacher added to my feelings of differentness. When we had dances at school, he would make the boys dance with the girls. But he wouldn't make anyone dance with me.

In the eighth grade our school held a dance for which a queen and two princesses were to be chosen. I was popular enough, I felt, that there was hope for me to be selected—probably not as the queen but possibly as one of the princesses. When I wasn't chosen, I was as devastated as the others who thought they might win . . . and didn't. I, though, blamed the outcome entirely on my disability. I went home, cried hysterically, and decided that no one would ever love me, no one would ever want to marry me. I realized that the brace and the crutches were symbols to the world that marked me as stupid, fat, dumb, and ugly.

I studied hard in high school to compensate for how badly I felt about myself; academics was one area in which I could excel. I kept all my feelings inside, didn't date much, and withdrew almost totally. Again, I lived for my vision of the future, when I hoped things would change for the better.

I went immediately to college, thinking that college would be different. The neat boys, I figured, would like the neat girls, but somebody—probably someone that no one else wanted—would like me. One day, though, when I wasn't included in a party invitation, the hurt returned and I retreated even further into my studies. Closeness with another was too threatening—it was too hard to trust another's caring for me. It wouldn't happen anyway. I didn't believe I deserved it.

When I was 24, I met Ken, a doctor who talked with me about how I experienced being disabled. This was the first time I talked openly about myself in this way. Until then, I had felt like I was carrying heavy weights on my shoulders. Ken lifted them, in part, simply by listening. I trusted him.

Ken was also a photographer and wanted to take pictures of me; he wanted to give me feedback on how I looked. I was terrified. Pictures would show my body. But with his encouragement, I finally agreed.

He took a series of 50 pictures of me, sitting and standing, with my brace on and off. In them, I looked so nervous, so upset when my legs could be seen. One horrible expression after another revealed how I was feeling. In one picture, though, Ken had caught me off guard; I was standing on my crutches without my brace. A broad smile covered my face. I was, I thought, radiant.

The photographs helped me to integrate the acceptable parts of me— my face and personality—with the major unacceptable part—my legs. I was starting to feel like I—not my legs—could take charge of my life. I had gotten a glimpse of my wholeness—skinny legs *and all*.

I remember fantasizing about being able to walk without my brace. In my fantasy, I could stand on my tip-toes, I could run up and down stairs. My spirit and joy burst forth. They were no longer constrained by my disability.

The task for me, then, was to somehow retain the vibrant freedom of my fantasy in the non-fantasy world, to understand that my disability was not the controlling force in my life.

I needed to know that I could be me, fully me, *with* a disability.

From grade school through college I had pushed myself hard, but always and only in academic areas where I could excel. I had left my body, my feelings, and my relationships with others unattended, behind. At 26, I took a year off from all the pushing. I needed to make sense of it all, to make sense of me.

I thought about relationships and careers, areas that my peers had been thinking about for 5 to 10 years. I knew I was behind. I moved into a group house and spent a lot of time talking to my six housemates about how they lived their lives, how they developed relationships and pursued career goals. I needed ideas, models of how to be (Should I be like him? Should I be like her?), and I felt that the information had to come from outside. I still didn't accept my own judgments. I wanted someone else to tell me what to do.

Ten months later, during a 2:00 a.m. rap in the kitchen, the realization suddenly struck; I would be disabled all my life. I would still be using my brace when I was 45, 55, and 65.

It's hard for me now to believe that I had succeeded in denying such a basic fact for so long. But while I was growing up, I was taught a lot about denial; polio was never discussed. So to me, for a long time, it was never really there.

My viewpoint now was changing in important ways. The vision of my non-disabled future was being replaced by reality.

I joined a self-help group called "Living with a Disability or Chronic Disease." Each participant, including the leader, had a disability. As we all talked, the similarities in our life experiences became apparent to me. I began to understand that society's messages were responsible for my self-hate. I began to separate who I was from the stigma of disability. That was the beginning of my opening myself up to the world.

I continued to clarify my ideas about careers and, in the fall of 1975, I took a counseling training course. Soon after, I found a job in the Disabled Student Center at the University of Massachusetts (Boston). For 2½ years, I worked there with students with disabilities. This experience launched my involvement as an advocate in the Disability Rights Movement.

While I was at the Disabled Student Center, a conference about disabled people and sexuality was scheduled in Boston. I was so excited that there was to be a conference about us! When I got there, however, I found that I was one of only five disabled people in the audience of 150, and that all of the presenters were able-bodied. I was furious. Women would never allow men to run a conference about women's sexuality. The conference marked the beginning of my political awareness about disability.

I continued counseling groups of disabled people and, in 1977, a core of individuals united in their concern for the rights of disabled people emerged. We soon incorporated as the Boston Self-Help Center, a counseling and advocacy organization run by and for disabled people.

One of our first advocacy efforts was directed at Friday's, a newly opened inaccessible restaurant. Eating there one night, I questioned the manager about his plans for access, and his answer showed little concern. "Don't worry about it," he said, "just bring your wheelchair friends, and we'll carry them in."

He soon learned that he should have been more careful in what he said to me. Three weeks later, I took 50 of my friends to lunch at Friday's; 13 of them were wheelchair users. In the name of the Boston Self-Help Center, we also invited one of the local television stations to join us.

Overwhelmed, the management immediately called its national headquarters for advice while my party of 50 waited. Finally, we were told that we could come in but that insurance company regulations absolutely forbid any of the restaurant staff from carrying us. We then simply assisted each other inside and had a terrific time. Our point had been effectively made, and soon the Architectural Barriers Board together with the Attorney General's office became involved.

We lost, ultimately, on a technicality. The building permit for Friday's had been issued on the same day that the Barriers Code became effective. But we gained enormously from the publicity and our sense of community spirit.

Others involved in the growing advocacy movement nationwide were adopting the same techniques. Protesters using wheelchairs found they were not arrested because local jails were inaccessible. A deaf man leading a rally in front of the White House pretended not to understand the policemen who were asking to see his parade permit. The policemen walked away in frustration, unaware that the deaf man was a skilled lipreader and that there were interpreters present to facilitate communication. These examples begin to suggest both the flavor and the effectiveness of the advocacy strategies I most enjoy. Indeed, the basic principle of acting outside of an adversary's experience still works for us.

My concerns with the issues of disability rights spurred me to get further involved in political action. I learned everything I could about our legal rights, especially those entitled under our Civil Rights Statute (Section 504 of the Rehabilitation Act of 1973). Soon I was conducting workshops on Section 504 from Maine to Virginia. Up and down the East Coast, I was connecting with disabled peers.

In the past 2 years, under the auspices of the Massachusetts Coalition of Citizens with Disabilities, I have developed and implemented the Project in Self Advocacy. The project enables us to provide funds to groups of people with disabilities around the state and to assist them in organizing on their own behalf.

Being involved in the disability rights movement has so far been the highlight of my career. Because the movement is attempting to resolve the critical issues facing people with disabilities, and because these issues relate to every aspect of a disabled person's life, I have found myself variously engaged in advocacy, organizing, counseling, legal work, lobbying, and media efforts. I have been challenged to develop and to use every bit of creativity, leadership, and intelligence within me. And I feel I've been effective in altering the stigma of disability.

I have forged a successful challenging career and have been able to offer myself as a positive model to others—a far cry from where I was only a few years earlier.

And I don't see myself as incredible or as a super-woman. I've taken what I am and have made it work for me. This, I believe, is life's challenge for everyone.

This past year has presented me with a new test of my strength and resourcefulness. I have become affected by post-polio syndrome, a set of symptoms characterized by fatigue, muscular weakness, and muscle pain. It is sometimes described as premature aging.

The medical profession theorizes that those nerve cells in the spinal cord that survived the initial attack of polio have since been overworking to compensate for the loss, and that they are now dying. Consequently, as the nerve impulses continually fail to reach the muscles, the muscles atrophy. This condition is just now showing up in people in their 30's and 40's, and it affects previously uninvolved parts of the body.

At times during the past 6 years, I had experienced recurring bouts of exhaustion lasting from 3 to 6 weeks. A year ago, though, when the exhaustion struck, it didn't go away. I have been tired every single day of this year. And for several months last winter, I felt dizzy every time I stood up, I was exhausted simply by walking into the kitchen, and I had to stop at every step when climbing the stairs. My symptoms have also included difficulty in concentrating, sleep disturbances, confusion, irritability, and depression.

Since these symptoms are related to many different conditions, I have spent more than a year reading and studying about them and questioning many doctors, examining a host of possibilities. I've seen a general practitioner, a hematologist, a gynecologist, a polarity therapist, an endocrinologist, an acupuncturist, a naturopath, and a psychiatrist. Not one of them could find anything physically wrong with me. I began to feel crazy.

My own research into my condition finally led me to discover the diagnosis of post-polio syndrome. Since doctors at the National Institutes of Health have been studying this syndrome for several years, I believe they can offer the best guesses about what's happening to me. I will be going there soon to participate in a national study designed to document the post-polio syndrome and to begin the search for a cure.

I have spent this difficult year trying to listen and respond to my body. I have learned that if I walk further than two or three blocks, I become exhausted and need to sleep. Indeed, any use of my legs, whether walking or standing, can now exhaust me. I have started to use a wheelchair at work.

I have learned as well that being outdoors, especially in the sun, is also exhausting, and now I have to be careful about participating in my favorite activities, swimming and sailing. I have learned that full-time work is too difficult—my tolerance for stress is dramatically decreased—and I have cut back to part-time. I have learned to come home every day after work and rest; often I find I am home for the night.

The rest of this condition, though, is still a mystery to me. This morning, for example, I awakened with pains in my legs, my upper arms, and my fingers. Why my arms and fingers? What did I do yesterday? Did I sleep in an uncomfortable position last night? What can I do today so that my fingers won't hurt tomorrow? Or is the pain going to increase on its own despite my best efforts? I spend much of each day pondering these kinds of questions, trying to care for myself.

This lack of being in control is becoming very hard to live with. I am used to planning my activities, setting goals, accomplishing tasks. But I can't predict my future anymore. Now, for example, I make my plans with the understanding that I may have to change them at the last minute.

A friend recently summarized my situation well: "Of course it's got to be the same thing that's haunted you all of your life. You've moved heaven and earth to learn to live with it, proudly, and then it goes and changes the rules."

Polio's back in the driver's seat and I don't like it. I don't want it.

When this new syndrome first struck, my friends were very supportive. But after a month or two, they began to feel guilty; they felt powerless to help. So I spent a lot of time alone, staring at the walls in my bedroom. I couldn't sleep, but I also couldn't move around or concentrate enough to read. Friends still invited me to go places with them, but I had to decline. I was just too tired.

I wanted people to spend time with me on my terms, to be willing to do things that I could comfortably do. I wanted them to come and sit with me, watch TV, talk, but not to expect much from me. I was reluctant to ask; I felt like I had nothing to offer in return.

For me to live my life like you enjoy living yours, you're going to have to change. Change your walking speed so I can keep up with you and not trail behind. Change your activities so you have an afternoon to visit with me. Change your steps, curbs, buses, and buildings so I can use them, too.

Don't expect me to change. I really can't.

I've begun the process of making my new illness work for me. I'm fighting the "more is better" principle and giving up being physically active—taking walks, swimming, biking. Now I'm focused and choosey about how I spend time. I pace myself and rest lots.

Also, I say "No" without feeling guilty. I have an unbeatable excuse. I've learned that I'm responsible for my needs and that I can ask for help to meet them.

Who's to say which kind of life is "more," which kind of life is "better"?

For people who are disabled, there is a systematic and confining set of cultural beliefs called "able-bodiedism." In my opinion, this set of beliefs is as pervasive as all the other "isms," all the other ways that individuals mistreat each other because of fear, lack of experience, and lack of information.

When I go out to shop in stores that I have never been in, or when I go to a party where there are people that I have never met, I am struck by the curious reactions to me—the stopping, the pointing, the looking, the looking away. I am eager to understand where these reactions are coming from, how people view me as a person, a disabled person, and, in particular, as a disabled woman.

There is also in able-bodiedism a message that disabled people are not sexual. I have been very awkward with my femaleness and extremely vulnerable to negative judgments by men. About 10 years ago, a man I was dating said he could never marry me because he wouldn't want to be seen walking down the street with a crippled woman. I believed him, and I was devastated.

Since I have always believed that I am not enough, that I am undeserving, it's hard for me to assert myself. It's also hard for me to get angry at people. Instead I try to please.

Recently, a friend told me that I smile a lot. Of course I do. I'm terrified that people will find out that I'm not feeling well and will desert me.

It's especially hurtful when someone who is disabled hurts me. I always hope for more understanding.

But we who are disabled do act out our prejudices on each other. We make judgments about degrees of disability and assume that people who are less disabled are somehow better. We believe the results of attitudinal studies that show some disabilities to be more socially acceptable; that being ambulatory, for example, is better than being a wheelchair user. We

believe that we are passive, powerless, guilty, ugly, stupid, and hopeless. As a result, we may try to pass as able-bodied. Or we may stay isolated in our homes.

In my work with groups, I see this stigmatizing among disabled peers happening often. In one group, for example, most of the members are deaf with varying degrees of vision. They will say that they are deaf, but they won't say that they are also blind. They will put off using a cane, actually endanger their lives, because they don't want to acknowledge their dual disability. They are afraid that they will be less acceptable if they are seen as more disabled.

In other groups, I have heard members say that they have no problems, that everything in their lives is fine. I know they have given up hope for anything better, or that they are unaware, perhaps afraid, of their needs.

I have been involved in the disability rights movement for more than 6 years. The community of disabled people provides a kind of safety for me. I feel like I have found my home.

I often dream of a country in which everyone is disabled. I got a glimpse of this in 1977 at the White House Conference on Handicapped Individuals. There were 4000 people there, 3000 of them disabled. I saw every kind of disability imaginable, including combinations of disabilities; people in wheelchairs using respirators and portable iron lungs; short deaf people; and blind wheelchair users. The experience was incredibly rich.

Throughout the 4 days that I attended, I was curious about all of our differences. I stared at people (I do it too!), fascinated by how peoples' bodies worked. I was completely awed by the variety.

I Would Be This Way Forever

When the conference was over, I went to a restaurant with a friend. I couldn't believe how boring it was to be in a place with people who all walked the same, sat the same, talked the same. None of them used their hands to talk, none had canes or dogs or wheelchairs or respirators. It was so boring to me. There was no wealth, no richness. I felt a loss.

At the White House Conference I had felt so free and flirtatious, so powerful and alive. This was my world and in it I could do anything. I wasn't afraid of judgments. I was in the majority. For a short while, at least, I could actually experience the goal toward which I am still working: to be completely proud about being disabled.

I think of the slogans of the women's movement—"The Sisterhood is Powerful"—and of the civil rights movement—"Black is Beautiful." Both describe very positive images. I have tried for years to develop a similar slogan for disabled people. I want one for us.

When I have asked people to list ten adjectives that describe disabled people, nine of the ten choices are usually negative. And the positive one is usually "inspiring." I am not depressed all of the time, nor am I inspiring. I am just a whole lot like you. The difference between us is not one of substance but one of degree.

If I were to meet me today, here is what I think I would notice. I would notice that I am friendly, warm, and open; that I make contact with people, look straight at them. I would notice that I am attractive, with dark curly hair, about shoulder length, and a beautiful smile; my eyes sparkle when I laugh, and I laugh a lot. I would see that I am generally reflective, a little shy, but at times very bold and gregarious. I would notice that I am smart and quick and that I obviously enjoy people. I would also notice that I am trim and thin, and that I wear a brace on my left leg. If I were outdoors, I would notice, too, that I use a crutch when I walk.

If *you* were to meet me today, I guess I don't know what you would notice. But I am sure your list would be ordered differently. More than likely, the brace or crutch wouldn't be the last thing you would see.

Chapter 7

Except for My Leg

Stephen Spinetto

*B*efore the accident, I had never thought about being disabled. As a kid, the only people I had ever seen with amputated limbs were those who begged for money in the Haymarket Square area of Boston. It annoys me now to think of those men who I passed regularly on my way to hockey practice. I really thought they represented what it was like to be disabled.

I must add that even now I feel odd writing about myself as "disabled" or "handicapped" or whatever other label one might put on me. Most times, I simply do not think of myself that way. My daily routine is quite ordinary for me, so to me, my life is normal; the disability is just there, largely forgotten.

Once or twice a year, perhaps, my prosthetic leg will kick up (pardon the pun), and then, suddenly, I am an official gimp complete with crutches and other symbols; I am what other disabled people call "temporarily able-bodied." But most of the time, I just proceed with my life—independently—occasionally needing some assistance.

In June of 1967, I was 17 years old, finishing my junior year in high school. A friend and I had gone to visit friends who owned a house by a southern New Hampshire pond. As we were casting off from the dock in a small boat, my friend suddenly yelled for me to jump quick! I turned to see the bow of a power boat only a few yards away, racing straight toward me, full blast. I don't know if I jumped out of the boat or if I was knocked out by the impact; it happened too fast. In any case, from the moment I hit the water I experienced everything in a kind of nightmarish slow motion. The keel of the power boat slammed into my back and pushed me down into the mud bottom of the pond. (I was fortunate that the impact forced my head down; otherwise the propeller would have run from head to toe instead of just across my legs.)

When I came to the surface, I was in pain; but I wasn't exactly sure where the hurt was coming from. The lower half of my body felt like it was on fire. I swam for the ladder at the end of the dock. When I reached it, I couldn't find the rungs with my feet; I remember thinking that the impact must have broken my back.

I climbed the ladder with my arms and, when I was out of the water, looked down to see one leg severed near the knee, turning on a string of tissue. My other leg, though not severed, was twisted at a strange angle and had a number of large slices cutting almost half way through. The pond was turning red.

It's funny what comes into your mind at times like this. When I first looked down at my legs, I was actually relieved that I wasn't paralyzed. Then I realized that my current state of affairs was none too good either. I was scared (more by the screams of my friends than by the sight of my legs) but, in a strange way, I was also calm.

When I reached the top of the ladder, I crashed face first onto the dock and, with the help of my friends, wrapped tourniquets around my legs. The boat that had struck me kept right on going.

With all the bleeding, I was convinced after only 15 minutes that I was dying; the ambulance took nearly an hour to arrive. On the way to the hospital the ambulance attendant, in an attempt to make me feel better, said, "Don't worry, after some stitches they'll probably send you home tonight."

I replied, "The only way I'm going to leave the hospital by tonight will be in a box."

The doctors tried to save the leg, but after a few days I was still running a very high fever and could smell the awful stench of gangrene. It came as little surprise when, 4 days after the accident, the doctors gave up and removed my right leg at the knee.

I don't remember having any strong emotional reactions. I remember feeling badly, but not overwhelmed. Everything seemed not to be real, like when a close friend or relative suddenly dies: you know it has happened, but you still expect to see that person walking into the room at any moment, smiling.

I kept thinking that, soon, I'll just get up and walk out of this place, and I carefully avoided thinking of things too far off into the future. First things first, I figured, like getting out of the hospital, having the pain stop, having the damn needle routines come to an end.

In my private moments, I remember thinking that I still might die . . . and that I hadn't really gotten started on living.

I was treated exceptionally well during my more than 2-month hospital stay. The only exception I recall is the many false promises made with good intentions. For example, I was told that the artificial leg I would receive would look absolutely real, that it would even have hair on it, toes, the whole works. Having never seen one before, I believed it. When I finally saw what I would be walking on, though, I was seriously disappointed. Here I was, expecting something lifelike, something that you simply slip on—and that's that. Instead, I got this pink plastic thing that hurt like hell, which, with all of its straps and belts, would never be mistaken for anything real.

I was told a lot of bullshit by medical professionals who should have known better. I could have taken the truth. I certainly would not have had as hard a time adjusting to the new leg if I hadn't been expecting something so much better.

While still in the hospital, I realized that sooner or later I would have to go out in public without my leg. The thought shook me. I don't like being stared at; even my first short trips out into the relative safety of the hospital corridors were difficult.

I took one of the first ventures out of my hospital room with my high school girlfriend. I was in a wheelchair, she was pushing. About 50 feet down the hall, we encountered a group of people on their way to visit another

patient. An older woman, upon seeing me, stopped in her tracks and yelled, "Look at that kid with only one leg." I thought I would die on the spot. It may seem incredible, but nothing else that has happened to me since has had such a deep and devastating impact.

That same woman visited a nearby patient daily. After a week of thinking about what she had done, I made a decision to retaliate: if she was going to continue to stare, I would really give her something to stare at. My girlfriend brought me a winter glove that I attached to my pajamas at the end of my stump. Later, as I passed the staring lady, I waved my new hand to her. She almost passed out. My girlfriend and I returned to my room where I laughed so hard that the stitches in my leg began to throb.

I was released from the hospital at the end of August to begin an outpatient program of physical therapy at a Boston rehabilitation center (paid for by the insurance company of the woman operating the power boat). There, I was to find people who were generally 10 to 20 years older than I and who had lost limbs mostly as a result of industrial accidents. In my opinion, it is much harder to adjust to a disability when you are older than when you are young. And some of the men at the center did not appear to be adjusting very well at all. Most of them would never be able to go back to their old jobs; for these blue-collar men, future employment opportunities would be very limited.

It wasn't until I came to the rehabilitation center that I had ever felt at all disabled. There, suddenly, I saw all these other people, some with a disability just like mine. Still I thought, "I can't really be like them." They seemed handicapped. They needed help to get around. They complained loudly and often. They sat around in bathrobes and played cards endlessly. They practiced arts and crafts in the occupational therapy department (and reminded me of overgrown children at summer camp).

At noon every day I was picked up at school and spent the rest of the afternoon at the center. This schedule continued for 7 months and caused me to miss a considerable number of classes. During Christmas vacation I received what is called a pylon leg, something in which I was immediately disappointed. As had been the case at the hospital, I had earlier been given the impression that this new leg would simply be attached and would then enable me to go running off. I should have known better. I wasn't ready for the pain that it caused, for the difficulty I encountered in learning how to walk on it, or for how alien and heavy it first felt.

At the rehabilitation center, I realized that people other than myself would be setting limits for me, that I might lose control of my life. Although no one ever told me I couldn't do certain things or that I shouldn't expect to be able to do what I could before, there was no encouragement for me to explore for myself what I *could* do. And around me, all I could see were crippled people whose lives seemed to have come to a close.

Becoming disabled at a relatively young age does have certain advantages. Not yet married, for example, I didn't have to worry if my wife would still love a man who was no longer whole (isn't that what happens in all the movies about people who lose limbs?). And since, at 18, I was at an important turning point in my life—no longer a kid, not yet an adult—it was easier for me to fold this new situation into my developing life-style and go on from there. I am sure it would have been much harder to adapt if I were older, if I were already set in my adult ways.

I was, however, forced to make some decisions about my life much sooner than I would have had I not lost my leg. College? Career? At the time, I thought that my options for future employment would be confined to the desk job category, an option reinforced by just about everyone around me—from my high school guidance counselor to my parents. This must have been their way of making sure I went on to college.

At the doorway to my parents' house, the adult world always came to an end. No matter that I was regarded by most everyone who knew me as a mature person, as someone who was working out a difficult problem with good success, in the house, I had become a preschooler. For the first several months after leaving the hospital, I was hardly allowed to leave this domestic time warp except to go to school or to rehab therapy. I was being protected from something, especially by my mother. I wasn't exactly sure from what.

My father knew I was looking forward to learning to drive again; he understood that getting back into a car represented an important symbol of liberation to me. And he agreed to help. He had been advised, though, by some of his police friends that my license would now be subject to certain restrictions, so we went to the registry to learn what these would be. That's when we discovered that because I had lost my leg, my license had been revoked (to this day I'm not sure how they knew). It would be necessary, we were informed, for me to take the driving test again.

On Sundays, my father took me to the local shopping center, and there, in the empty parking lot, I re-learned how to operate a car . . . with my prosthetic leg on the gas pedal and my good leg on the brake.

In the spring I passed the driver's test with ease. An automatic transmission and a hand-operated dimmer switch were the only restrictions imposed, and since the family car was already equipped this way, I was ready to roll. Then, 2 months later on my 19th birthday, my driver's license expired.

When I went to have it renewed at the Registry, the woman behind the counter took it and disappeared—for a long time. When she finally returned, she informed me that since my license had been revoked the year before, I should have returned it then. I could see what I was getting into now. I tried to review the sequence of events with her: that I had, in fact, turned in my license when it was revoked; that I had taken and passed a new driver's test; that my license had been returned by the Registry; and that because it had expired, it now simply needed to be renewed.

Her response sounded as if it came from the Registry's book of frustrating procedures; she insisted that the Registry would never let me drive using my prosthetic leg for the gas pedal and my left foot for the brake. And she supported her insistence by pointing out the absence of any records to indicate that I had, in fact, re-taken the driver's test.

To make a long story—the kind that always seems to come from the Registry—short, I was required to take the driver's test once again. And once again, I passed. There are even official records now that say so.

I can't believe that the Registry would give a drunk driver as much difficulty as it gave to me. Indeed, the woman who had been operating the power boat was, herself, suspected of being drunk, and she had her license to operate a boat revoked for only 1 year. Mine, on the other hand, had been revoked with the possibility of my never getting it back again.

Dealing with bureaucracies has, without exception, been the most difficult of my experiences since returning from the hospital. Let me tell you briefly about two others that tried their hardest to make my life miserable.

Shortly after I was released from the hospital, I received notice to report to the draft board. The Vietnam War was in full swing at the time, killing off some of my high school friends. My prosthetic leg was still months away, so I arrived at the appointed time on crutches, pant leg tied up. I hardly looked like material for the special forces.

The woman who seemed to be in charge treated me as if I were some kind of super draft evader. I tried to explain to her that I really hadn't performed an amputation on myself in order to evade the draft or to avoid getting shipped to Vietnam just to save myself the trouble of getting it blown off.

Nonetheless, she made me sit down and answer every one of the questions on the intake form. She actually sat there, with her straight face aimed right at my empty pant leg, and asked: "Will this disability be of lasting duration?"

A few weeks later, the results of my meeting were mailed to my home: I was classified 1-Y. In other words, I could be drafted only in emergency situations. I figured this was probably safe; if things ever got so bad that I was needed in the armed forces, chances of my making it from my house to the draft board without getting blown to bits would likely be slim.

It's interesting to note that 2 years later, my apartment roommate—a macho, football player type—received a 4-F classification from the same draft board. He had a trick knee and would never be drafted. I had a stump where my knee ought to be and could be drafted in emergency situations. His family was relatively wealthy, mine relatively poor.

Coming from a working-class background, if I was going to go to college it would be up to me to come up with the money. Before the accident, my plan was to get a scholarship either through sports or through the Naval ROTC. The possibility of either ended in the New Hampshire pond.

While I was in the hospital, however, I was visited by my high school guidance counselor who informed me that the Massachusetts Rehabilitation Commission would provide for my education. This sounded great! All I had to do was to take a battery of exams and then the funds for college would be made available.

Most of the exams were of the IQ and aptitude type. I was also sent to a psychiatrist to see, I guess, if losing my leg had also made me crazy. With his mustache and his thick German accent, the shrink seemed to me to be imitating either Sigmund Freud or Adolph Hitler. His endless questions focused initially on whether I liked my parents, and, as they continued, they grew increasingly irrelevant. "Vot vould you prefer," he asked in all seriousness, "to paint zee fence or to paint zee barn?" (Remember, *I* was the one being evaluated here.) I told him, in fact, that I hated painting anything, and at this his mustache began to twitch, and he wrote even more furiously on his note pad.

Eventually, he concluded that I did not need rehabilitation, that I was probably the same as I was before the accident—except for my leg, of course—and that my career goals—to be an architect—had remained unchanged. Sounded to me like a pretty good report, at first; then I learned that as a result of this evaluation, I was uneligible for rehabilitation funds. As it was explained to me, if I had wanted to be a steel worker, then perhaps the Commission could rehab me into a clerk or an office worker; that's the kind of thing that's done all the time. But I wanted to be an architect, before the accident and after. So, according to the rehab commission, there was nothing for them to rehab me into. They would have to change me in order to fund me. The only alternative for eligibility was if I was found to be clinically crazy or suicidal due to the loss of my leg. Again it turned out that a promise made to me in the hospital proved not to be true.

Immediately after the accident, what bothered me most of all was the prospect of not participating in athletics again. I was sure that this option was now closed. In high school, I had played on both the hockey and the tennis teams; I was no star, but I enjoyed playing immensely. The prosthetist fit my leg for hockey skates, and I found that I could skate quite well. The only difficulty I had was in getting up from a fall; I couldn't get my prosthetic foot flat enough on the ice to hold an edge.

My old high school uniform was given back to me, but I was not allowed to play; the school's insurance company made sure of that. As for tennis, I found that I couldn't move fast enough to play nearly as well as I once had. Frustrated, I gave it up.

I had always participated in sports for one reason: they were enjoyable. After the accident, tennis and hockey, at least, no longer satisfied that criterion.

I pursued no athletics for the next 2 years. I just wasn't sure about what I could or could not do. My body image was low and sinking. Then, while studying at the Boston Architectural Center, I met a beautiful woman from North Carolina. She was 5 years older, and much more sophisticated than I. I fell in love immediately.

She was a skier, and, soon after I met her, she and her roommate took a weekend trip to Vermont while I stayed home and studied. When she returned she reported on the trip in enthusiastic detail. That's when I decided that if she was going skiing, then I was going skiing, too.

Our first weekend in Vermont was at Glen Ellen-Sugar Bush. I went to the ski school desk, explained that I had only one leg and that I wanted to learn to ski. Ironically, one of the instructors had recently broken his leg racing and was skiing that weekend with one ski (with his other leg in a cast). My first lesson—using regular ski poles and one ski—was brutal. I was black and blue from top to bottom, particularly the bottom. I was sore all over but I had the best time I've had in years. I was back to sports.

A short time later, I heard about a group of disabled people who skied at the Haystack ski area in southern Vermont. They used small skis—outriggers—attached to forearm-type crutches. The program of free lessons and free skiing in which they participated was sponsored by an organization called The New England Handicapped Sportsmen Association. After a few lessons at Haystack using the outrigger, I was skiing well.

Every year at Winter Park, in the Rocky Mountains of Colorado, a national organization of disabled skiers holds its national races. I took my first trip there in 1974 with a group of people from the New England Association. This was my first involvement with any disabled group, and the experience floored me. Roughly 150 disabled skiers gathered together from all over the country. There were doctors, lawyers, military officers, politicians, constructions workers—people from all walks of life. I have never seen a group of people with less inhibitions about their disabilities. They were absolutely outrageous. Some used peg legs and looked like they stepped out of a pirate story. Many walked around in shorts with their prosthetic legs brightly painted in a variety of colors.

As a group, these characters presented a stark contrast to the image of disabled people I had fashioned from my experiences in the Rehabilitation Center. Having been so close to death, the members of this gang clearly appreciated that they were alive. Indeed, they seemed intent on confirming their vitality, their exuberance, at every opportunity.

Each night, the local bars offered free beer to those participating in the races. During my first stint in one of these bars, I watched a group of people taking turns chugging beer out of a prosthetic leg.

Prior to this trip to the Rocky's, I hadn't felt comfortable at a beach and would never wear shorts no matter how hot the weather. I was embarrassed by people's stares. Being an amputee made me feel very different from other people. After Colorado, it seemed normal to be disabled.

I can still remember one of my first runs from the top of a mountain in Colorado, 12,000 feet high. I was one of the first skiers up the lift in the morning. The day was brilliant, sunny. When I reached the run that I wanted to take, I was alone; the view across some of the highest peaks in the country was breathtaking. This was the most silent moment I have ever known. Skiing down the mountain, in big wide turns through fresh snow, I felt like I was flying.

To most disabled people, the sensation of speed is never experienced; even those who are able to run cannot run very fast. For this reason, primarily, I found skiing to be an incredible high. It offered me a feeling of freedom that I couldn't achieve any other way.

Skiing has had a huge impact on my life. It gave me much needed confidence—and pride—in myself. I was able to excel at a sport that many able-bodied persons cannot do (when I had two legs, I had been afraid to try). I think it's important for everyone to excel at some physical activity. But for a disabled person, proficiency in a sport that requires such physical skill is even more rewarding.

The confidence that came with learning to ski spilled over into other areas of my life. I found I was able to deal more effectively with others; I became less inhibited about looking strange if that's what it took to respond to a new challenge. I also realized that I could do anything I really wanted to do; my self-doubt was easing. Since learning to ski, for example, I have participated in organized squash, weightlifting, and many other sports. The motto of the ski program is, I guess, particularly appropriate to me: "If I can do this, I can do anything."

It would have been so much better, I believe, if people hadn't gone out of their way to be so nice to me after the accident. I really didn't want to be treated so differently. At times, in fact, the treatment of others proved embarrassing. Our local State Representative, for example, insisted on having a sign placed in front of my house that read: "CAUTION: CRIPPLED CHILD." That sign made me wonder whether I was being protected from the cars or whether the people in the cars were being protected from seeing me.

My parents also arranged to have a van pick me up at home and bring me to school during my senior year, a special service that was suggested by the school department. I had told my parents that I'd rather ride the regular school bus with my friends, but after I saw how many people were going out of their way to make this special arrangement work, I decided to try the van—for them. The first time I rode it was also the last. Not only was I the oldest student in the van, I was also the only one who wasn't mentally handicapped. The entire ride was totally out of control with kids screaming, jumping, and hollering throughout. When we arrived at school, I left as fast as my crutches allowed. I went home that day on the regular bus.

My high school was housed in a large five-story building. Fortunately it had an elevator. Unfortunately, as the elevator was used mainly for supplying the cafeteria on the fifth floor, it was never in much of a hurry. As I became more proficient with my crutches, I found it much easier to bypass this "convenience" altogether in favor of the stairs.

I was tremendously surprised by the overwhelming support that my family and I received after the accident. When I needed blood, for example, it seemed that everybody I knew—and many whom I'll never know—donated. I received sacks of mail filled with get well cards, and carloads of friends regularly drove the 40 miles from Cambridge to visit me. Because I was in a Catholic hospital, the rules about visitors were strictly enforced; somehow, though, the staff always found a way to bend them for me.

The support continued after my hospitalization. Whenever there was a school party or dance, I was always called by a number of friends asking if I needed a ride. When you're an adolescent, peer support like I received can seem even more important than family support.

I was particularly relieved to learn that my disability didn't seem to mean a whole lot to my friends; mostly, I was relieved to learn that it didn't mean a whole lot to the girls.

When I graduated in June, I signed up for a summer school class in architecture at Harvard University's Graduate School of Design. Practically everyone in the course was a graduate student, and I was, most of the time, intimidated. Nonetheless, the class was excellent, providing me with a solid introduction to architectural design as well as with an "A" for the course. Encouraged by my success, and with some help from the instructor, I landed an office boy position at the Architects Collaborative, the well-known firm of Walter Gropius. At the same time I began attending the evening school of the Boston Architectural Center.

My job required me to hustle around a five-story office building delivering mail and supplies. There was only one elevator, and I was constantly on my feet. To my surprise, however, all the running around—up and down the stairs all day long—affected neither my leg nor my job performance. The two-legged office boys, I discovered, had nothing on me.

Several months into the job, a position opened up at one of the firm's construction sites, and the supervisor asked if I were interested in it. The partners, though, were wary as the building was a high-rise research laboratory and the job would require my climbing it to inspect the ongoing work. Finally, with some intervention by my direct boss, I was given the position as assistant to the construction supervisor—on a trial basis.

I found I had no problems negotiating the construction site. Well, I had one. I was asked to inspect some concrete forms at the top of the growing structure. At this point, the building was ten stories tall, and the stairs went only to the sixth. After that, it was all ladders, and, on the top two stories, these were on the exterior of the building. This meant that I would be roughly 80 feet in the air when I swung out onto the ladder.

As I started up the rungs, my prosthetic foot snapped off at the ankle. Fortunately, I didn't have my full weight on it and was able to hang onto the ladder, watching my foot, with its sock flailing in the breeze, fall to the ground.

The construction workers who helped me down were totally freaked out, especially the one who was behind me on the ladder and saw my foot sail right past his face.

When the construction was completed, I took time off and traveled to France, alone. I was a little worried about being so far from home, knowing not one other person. Mostly, though, I was concerned that something might go wrong with my leg, and that I would, in a very real sense, get stuck.

As it turned out I did a tremendous amount of hiking, especially in the French Alps where I would walk from one village to another through mountain passes. It was an especially beautiful experience, one that could not have been matched by the easier motorized alternative. Even with my stump bleeding at night, I felt it was worth it.

I was staying on the Left Bank of Paris in a small, family-owned hotel. One morning, the maid opened the door, and seeing me in bed, she immediately left. Later, though, when I was on the way out, the owner stopped me and demanded to know who else was staying in the room with me. The maid, he said, reported seeing another person's leg under the bed. My

French being rather poor, it was difficult and embarrassing to explain that it was I who was both on top of and, at the same time, under the bed.

Thousands of miles from home, the trip to France represented the first time I was totally on my own. I returned a different person. I was able to cope easily with the everyday problems my leg causes. And I was never again nervous about being alone, with just me to depend upon.

Since the accident, I have been frightened whenever I've been on the water. This is, perhaps, an understandable fear, but it's also one that was most frustrating; I loved sailing, and the fear didn't allow me to enjoy it. Even after spending a summer as a crew member on a racing boat, I still found myself nervous when called upon to handle a boat on my own.

This summer, my wife and I were invited to spend a weekend sailing in Maine with some friends who had chartered a boat for 2 weeks. On Saturday, we sailed out of Camden to Pulpit Harbor on the Island of North Haven. I was a passenger most of the way and was really nervous, particularly when the wind picked up to gusts of 35 to 40 knots. But we made it to Pulpit Harbor relatively smoothly.

We had a wonderful night at anchor and greeted the foggy August morning with slight hangovers. We waited out the mist over breakfast, and started back to Camden mid-morning. In light winds and a rolling sea, our sail proved easy. I handled the boat from the moment the sails were up until we reached Camden, a trip of about 5 hours duration. The rest of the crew were either below or asleep on deck with music plugged into their ears.

When we reached Camden, the sky had cleared and the wind picked up briskly. Normally in these conditions I would have handed the helm over to anyone rather than attempt to sail into the crowded busy harbor myself to find the mooring. But no one on the crew would take it. "You take it in," my friends said, "and do it under sail. Let's not motor in."

I weaved into the inner harbor, spotted a mooring, and put the boat right on it. After the boat was secured and we opened some beers, I realized what I had accomplished. I had sailed from Pulpit Harbor to Camden—on my own. The only emotion I felt was joy. The fear was gone.

In February 1978 a surprise blizzard buried eastern Massachusetts under 3½ feet of snow. Coastal communities were devastated by wind and waves; in the Town of Scituate alone, more than 800 families lost their homes. The Governor declared a State of Emergency and ordered all businesses closed until the highways could be cleared. Since I worked for the Commonwealth, I was called in to help the newly homeless families find temporary housing.

At the end of that long first day, I headed for the subway with several others from the Disaster Relief Team. One of the others was Alice, the woman in charge of our operation.

We found an open restaurant in Harvard Square and were soon in the middle of dinner, drinks, and warmth when Alice's husband arrived to walk her home. Strangely, though, he waited for her outside, in the blowing snow, preferring not to join the rest of us. Alice was clearly embarrassed by her husband's awkward stance, and our good mood was dented. It was easy to see that all was not well with Alice's marriage.

Gradually, through the spring and early summer, Alice and I became closer. Somehow, for example, we always managed to bump into each other on the way out the office; every evening we rode the subway home together. Because she was married, though, we both worked hard at keeping some distance between us. I was nonetheless falling in love.

Late one Friday afternoon, I stopped at Alice's office to see if she wanted some subway company. I also took the opportunity to brag a little about a concert I was planning to go to that weekend. She was immediately envious, and, when I told her that I'd have been happy to take her if she hadn't been married, she informed me that she and her husband had, in fact, been separated for almost 4 months.

This new knowledge just about ruined my weekend. All I could think of was that my date wasn't—and could have been—Alice.

Following the weekend, Alice and I had dinner together often. But she would always say good night to me in the Square and walk home alone.

One night, we were having drinks at the Harvest Restaurant, and I suggested that we stay for dinner. Alice surprised me by suggesting that we prepare dinner at her house instead. From that evening on, Alice and I were inseparable. Three weeks later we were living together—sort of. Alice still wouldn't admit that we were serious. A serious relationship, she said, wasn't part of her plan just yet.

That September, Alice began looking for a new apartment. I had been hoping that she'd move into mine and didn't quite know what to make of

her searching for another. So I was devastated when she returned one afternoon and announced that she had bought a new house.

Alice asked me to examine the new house for her, and, since it was not too far from my own (and since she seemed so excited about it), I reluctantly agreed. And I was greatly surprised. Her new house was small—only three rooms and three floors—and had been built somewhere between 1755 and 1795. Alice's new house was one of the oldest in Boston.

A month later, we moved into it together. And on October 18, 1980, Alice and I were married.

Nothing now could make my life more complete.

Chapter 8

The Something That Happened Before I Was Born

Marsha Saxton

*A*lthough I was born with the second most common birth defect, wore braces on my legs, and had a great deal of surgery, my recognition of myself as a disabled person still, at 31, feels new. Sometime in the first trimester of my mother's pregnancy something happened (genetic? nutritional? perhaps astrological?), and the development of my tiny spine was disrupted. That place on my spine never grew together, and I was born not quite finished.

This something-that-happened is called spina bifida, and it left me with weakness in my legs and feet and with a bladder that doesn't work quite right. The severity of spina bifida varies considerably. Some babies are born with no brain at all, others grow up never aware of the small niche somewhere in their spine. Many, as they get older, use wheelchairs and long leg braces. I walk with a slight limp and my legs are thin. I catheterize my bladder several times a day.

When I tell people that I have spina bifida, I'm sometimes told how lucky I must feel to be able to walk so well. I puzzle at this view. (I've never been told how unlucky I am for being disabled at all.) It's as if I were slated to be disabled, but somehow got off easy with a light sentence. As I see it, I'm not lucky or unlucky. I'm just the way I am.

But I'm not disabled, I always thought. Or handicapped. And I'm certainly not that other word—*crippled*.

Several years back, I was working as a speech therapist in a chronic care hospital. The work was hard. My case load consisted mostly of people with stroke, late stages of degenerative disease, and serious head injury. Occasionally I would enter a patient's room armed with pictures, books, and adaptive communication devices ready for a session of communication therapy. The bed would be stripped. The patient had died. The other staff, over-case loaded as I, tried hard to counter my rising burnout; they could not, though, provide enough support. I decided to seek a support group, outside the hospital, for health professionals.

Not long after, something turned up in an organization called Boston Self Help Center. This small, newly formed group of counselors and disabled advocates offered, among other things, a "supervision group" for professionals working with disabled clients.

I pondered joining the group. This organization, after all, was for disabled people, and I felt only marginally included in that category. Perhaps I had been disabled as a child, but now I walked with just a slight limp. And as for my bladder not being normal, well, hardly anyone knew. Was I "disabled"?

I joined the supervision group. Over the weeks, our discussions of patients and of work stress gave way to a focus on our own personal histories. I began to look not just at how my patients made me feel but at what old pains, what unresolved feelings were getting touched off. How were the circumstances of my patients reminding me of my own self? Hospitalization. Dependence. Pain. Stigma. I began to confront the huge impact that being born disabled had upon who I am.

That was 6 years ago. These pages will share some of what I've learned.

What affected me most as a disabled child, I think, was being in the hospital so much. For several months every 2 years or so, I would go in for more surgery on my legs. I remember the feeling of dread when the letter from Shriner's Hospital arrived to announce my scheduled intake. Shriner's Hospital for Crippled Children, a charity hospital funded by wealthy businessmen and the East-West Football Game ("Strong legs run so that weak legs may walk") accepted me as a patient, though my parent's income was on the borderline of their income limits. We never could have afforded my surgeries without help.

I recall sitting in the rocker, my mother crying. I felt as if a big hand were reaching into our family to pluck me out. My parents seemed powerless; there was nothing they could do to prevent my leaving.

I remember, too, how little attention was paid to the surgery happening to help my legs work better. At the time, especially when I was young, that just seemed like a ruse to obscure what I knew was really true: my body was defective and so I had to be punished.

The hospital seemed to me like an orphanage. The other children seemed so disconnected from wherever they came; like me, they had been plucked from their homes to come to this place, "my second home," as my father called it. I was there during the 1950s and early 1960s, but the decor was of the 1920s and 1930s. On the wall murals, girls in ruffled bonnets and pantaloons and boys in nickers rolled wooden hoops. Our metal beds and high-sided cribs, even the night tables, were from that same era. The big TV's, one in each twelve-bed ward, were the only evidence of my own time.

My memories of the days there are of waiting, waiting for the surgery to happen. I was sometimes there for a month before the surgery was scheduled to occur.

In my earliest stays, before age 6, the hospital allowed no visiting at all. They told my parents that this policy prevented the spreading of germs, but even at my young age, I realized they simply wanted to minimize contact, to keep our ward world separate from the one we knew outside. The children would have cried and complained, felt lonely and afraid, if their parents had been able to come in and hold them. Such was the hospital mentality in those days of the early 1950s; it was still a time to keep children passive and silent.

The families of patients gathered on Sunday afternoons outside the windows of our rooms. Inside, we'd try to talk through the screened openings. I vividly remember peering down at my parents and my brother 15 feet below. I would try to smile and reassure them I was fine. My mother looked like she was about to burst into tears, and my father, behind his stories of what had been happening at home, looked nervous. My brother almost always looked puzzled.

Years later, in college, I read an article about the profound impact of lengthy parent-child separation on the emotional health of young children. I felt a pang of envy for those children whose mothers now stay overnight in the hospital with them, and I wondered about the hidden damage to my psyche.

The hospital conducted a kind of school for us, run by retired teachers and volunteers. We were given readers and math books and sat behind desks modified for wheelchairs. Classes consisted only of our reading lessons and answering questions on what we read. There were no open group discussions like those I enjoyed in my school at home. I always felt way behind at my school when I returned.

We also had crafts, which I enjoyed the most, partly because the volunteers in this class seemed more like the people I knew in my own world, and also because I loved the projects. We made lanyards, copper foil plaques, yarn dolls, and the like. In addition, I was given the privilege of using the sewing machine that belonged to the "Gray Ladies," a Red Cross volunteer group of elderly women who made the clothes we wore. (We weren't allowed to bring our own clothes or possessions.)

The Gray Ladies taught me how to knit and, while I waited for my surgery, I made many hats, scarfs, and vests. Then, during the longer time to heal and go home, I made more. It was only recently that I've been able to identify the feeling I get now, so many years later, when I pick up my knitting; it's a feeling of anxious waiting.

Sometimes the hospital had parties where clowns passed out ice cream and balloons and a man played the accordion or the piano. We sang, played bingo, and generally succeeded in making the room come alive. Then the party people would leave, and the wards seemed even emptier.

Unlike many of the children in the hospital, I could walk. As a result, during the waits for my surgery to be scheduled, I developed a game that was to set a life pattern for me. I would get things for others (comic books from the shelf) and fetch objects that had fallen from beds. I pretended I was a nurse, sometimes a doctor.

A patient in the hospital has a low status in our society; I opted for a higher one. I made myself a helper, someone with a purpose, a needed person. In my game, I created a reason for me to be. I was there to help the nurses clear the bed stands for the lunch trays, to fold the blankets, to fill the water glasses. I wandered around the ward and visited the other girls, the patients, asking them about themselves. "Did it hurt?" I'd ask. "Was there anything I could do?"

This game also took my mind off my loneliness, distracted me from my fear, and made me feel special. Sometimes the aides let me come into the kitchen and preview the dinner menu. Or I was allowed to accompany a nurse on an errand to the administrative offices. The nurses liked me a lot, and when I would return a couple of years later, many immediately recalled my smile and sunny disposition.

I have a vivid memory of a nurse saying to me in earnest, "God made you pretty and sweet to make up for your being crippled." I listened to this and guessed it must be true, but still I puzzled at my images of some of the other children there, scarred from burns or drooling from cerebral palsy, who apparently hadn't received the same compensation. Why was I handicapped and still pretty? It seemed a contradiction to my child's mind.

The word *crippled* was ugly and repulsive. Could I be hiding my real self? What a remarkable deception! These thoughts sometimes haunted my childhood.

The scariest part of the hospitalization for me was not the surgery, but the doctor rounds. On the mornings when these rituals were scheduled, the nurses and aides awakened us much earlier than usual. Meals and wash-ups were rushed. Those of us who were up for discussion would be dressed in white canvas bikinis that exposed our bodies.

Then they would come, the surgeons, the residents, the interns. All men. On rare occasion, a woman physical therapist accompanied them, but, like the nurses, she stood in back, out of the way, and never spoke unless she was asked for information.

They entered our ward, about 15 adults, trailing a big x-ray viewing box with racks underneath for charts. One by one, we'd be discussed, some of us just briefly. Strange long words were uttered; bandages were opened and quickly closed. Our bones showed purple on the x-ray screen.

Others of us would be dealt with in detail, with great deliberation as to how our bodies could be changed and improved. I was often discussed in depth, such an interesting case, this spina bifida who could walk without braces, though slightly wobbily; whose bladder retained urine quite well, but needed to be catheterized; who was quite bright (no signs of hydrocephalus or subsequent retardation).

I was told to walk up and down the ward, naked in my white bikini, as the doctors watched and talked and pointed to the bones on the screen and the bones in my body. One would call me over to him and he'd flex my feet up and down, and command me to stand on my toes, to stand on one foot, to bend my knees. How hard I'd try to do it right, so maybe they'd leave my body the way it was. Maybe they wouldn't make me have surgery.

Once, a surgeon—the one who looked so stern—called me over and poked at my hips. I was alarmed; until now, this place on my body had always been left untouched. My hips, I thought, were okay as they were. The surgeon began to untie my bikini, and a flood of terror rushed through me. Would I be even more exposed to this crowd?

It was rare for me, the brave crippled child, to show or even to feel my fear. I had learned to retain my power by *not* expressing my rage or showing my tears. I wouldn't let them scold me or shame me for resisting their orders.

But now in this group, my fear took control and, shaking, I grasped at the cloth and stared up at the surgeon. Pleading-eyed, I begged him to let me keep this token of privacy. Miraculously, he let go. A nurse stepped over and wrapped a robe around me, closing the scene like a curtain. The surgeon and the rest moved on. I swallowed tears and marvelled at not being scolded.

My recollection of surgery is a dreamlike blur: being wheeled into the operating room, the green masked people speaking with no mouths. I tried to stay awake as long as I could, talking and asking furiously. I was never told beforehand what was going to happen to me; I was only given reassurances that I would be all right.

Hours later, I would awake. Fighting the numbness, I would peer down at my legs to see the white casts propped way up high on pillows. I'd recognize the toes peeking out of the bandages, pink from Merthiolate. Bottles of fluid, some red, some clear, hung over me, feeding tubes in my arms. I always woke up alone.

And always there was a stuffed animal placed in my bed, a gift from the hospital. I would stare at it, trying to be pleased at the dog or bear or rabbit, but also fighting the temptation to cry that was prompted by the safety of this new friend (who, unlike grown-up people, could really see what I was feeling).

And then I would call out for the nurse. A little later, she'd appear, almost invariably with needle in hand; she was assuming I'd choose the numbness over the pain and awareness. At this point, I would call into play one of the many tricks I'd developed to exert the small degree of child power I could: I would ask for food. Not because I wanted to eat, but because hunger, to the nurses, was a sure sign that I was okay. They wouldn't try to drug me again for now. They'd be impressed with my quick recovery, and I'd be praised as a good patient.

My tactic also assured that the nurse would have to return, hopefully for as long as it took me to mouth the jello. I'd eat it and struggle through the druggy fog to ask the nurse questions that would keep her with me. My mouth would be dry, my throat aching from the trache tube, my tongue sore from the clamp used to keep me from choking. And still I talked. I never cried or complained of pain; that would have driven her away.

In all my hospital experiences, the saddest part was always the same. All those people trying so hard to help me: the nurses, the doctors, the volunteers, the Shriners. All of them hoping for me to get better and do well, all wanting to be kind and useful, all feeling how important helping me was. Yet never did anyone of them ask me what it was like for me. They never asked me what I wanted for myself. They never asked me if I wanted their help.

The surgery I had was very successful. Doctors I see now still comment on the skilled work. But I do not feel entirely grateful. I feel, instead, a remote anger stored beneath my coping pattern of complacent understanding. People do the best they can to help in meaningful ways, I know. I just wish all disabled children would say to their helpers: "Before you do anything else, just listen to me."

I believe my parents were somewhat unusual in the way they dealt with my disability. I think of my Mom, in particular, as courageous. She had to approach many different pediatric urologists before she could find one who would teach her to catheterize me (though nowadays this is often done). They berated her for her request, insisting that I would have to have an ileostomy or I'd die of infection.

My family didn't make a big deal of my being disabled. I was given responsibility appropriate for my age and was expected to help around the house and care for myself just like other girls. My mother's attitudes contributed to an ongoing theme in the relationships I was to develop with doctors as an adult: that of insisting on asserting my choices and accepting all medical advice as a wary consumer.

I was born before the days of parent groups and family services. My mother, therefore, found little support for the feelings she faced with a child who needed surgery often, got sick a lot and generally required close attention. I became her support. I was the one who listened to her. I was there when she cried, sometimes when she was crying about me.

Because of my bladder condition, I had to be near my mother all the time; I couldn't urinate without her there to catheterize me. This, in part, contributed to a strong pattern of dependence, maybe mutual dependence.

I cried when I'd pinch my finger, or when my cat died, but I never cried about being disabled. I came home from playing in the neighborhood once, and turned to my mother: "Mommy, they said I'm crippled!" Her eyes filled with tears. I must have studied her reaction and decided the best thing I could do was to reassure her that I wasn't hurting, that I was fine. I think I was 8 years old.

My early memories of my father remind me of the stereotyped daddies in children's books: a smiling friendly man in a suit, leaving for work. A musician and a teacher, my father worked nights and days, his way of dealing with the responsibilities of a family, a disabled child, and the pressures to succeed. But when he was home with us, he was the other kind of classic daddy: affectionate, kidding around, calling us funny names. He carried and held me a lot (restitution, I feel, for the isolation I'd felt in the hospital).

Once I remember sitting on his lap, he, home from work, wearing suit pants. My wayward and unpredictable bladder gave way and completely soaked him. His reaction, even to my 6-year-old perceptions, was a study in trying-not-to-show-your-feelings. He lifted me off, suggesting I ask Mommy to change me, and went off to change himself. I remember my embarrassment. I knew those pants would have to be dry cleaned, but I was never scolded for the inconvenience my special needs or problems may have caused. As a consequence, I didn't experience much of the "being

a burden" feelings with which so many of the disabled clients I've counseled still grapple.

My being disabled affected my brother. He'd had a sadness about him that, I've been told, started well before I was born. But my coming along, with all my needs for extra attention, my getting sick, needing surgery, needing to be carried and fussed over, maybe all that further fueled and complicated that sadness.

My parents tried not to let my disability lead to differential treatment, but I remember incidents slipping in, especially ones where well-intentioned relatives, feeling sorry for the cute little crippled one, lavished special favors. At a relative's Christmas reunion, I recall sitting amidst heaps of unwrapped dolls and games and dresses, and glancing across the room at my brother, who sat alone in a far corner, with his gifts: a book and a watch. The book, well below his advanced-for-his-age reading level, was no distraction for the resentment his face showed. I wonder, still, how much that resentment lingers; we're not as close as I wish we could be.

I went to school where my mom taught, so she could catheterize me during the day. There had been some resistance to my enrollment. My mother was told by the school nurse, "Well, you know, we don't have to take *them*!" All through school I was the only child with a visible handicap.

My differences were well accepted by the other children. I was rarely teased, and in fact, had a certain special status. My girlfriends would threaten the boys that if they were obnoxious, I might kick them with my braces!

An unfortunate incident stands out as one reason for my difficulty in sharing feelings with my peers. My pediatrician encouraged me to explain to my close friends about the differentness of my bladder. Until then, this was a secret I had carefully guarded. But I decided to take the advice. The girl I told promptly infiltrated the entire second grade with the information that I wore diapers. Aghast, I flatly denied it (it was, in fact, true), and the incident was soon forgotten by everyone but me. It took 10 years before I tried this kind of sharing again.

When I was 12, I was finished with most of the surgery and was able to stop wearing leg braces. I had looked forward to this for years. Now I could wear pretty shoes and not clump around in my heavy metal apparatus. I wouldn't, I thought, be seen as handicapped anymore.

I was overjoyed to wear sneakers to school on my first day back from the hospital. But I was met with a new concern, one I hadn't anticipated. A girl looked at my legs and said, "Wow, your legs sure are skinny. At least the braces hid that!" I was appalled to realize that removing the braces didn't make me normal. From then on until my 20's, I decided I wasn't ever going to let others see my differentness. I began to wear knee socks and pants whenever I could (even in hot weather). My favorite footwear was knee boots that successfully hid the skinniness of my legs. I avoided going swimming, which revealed the incision on my back and my slightly asymmetrical fanny. The risk of differentness was too great for my teenage self. I went underground as a disabled person.

It's funny how I react to comments or whistles from men in public. While most of my women friends, many of them feminists, react with annoyance or disgust to catcalls, I find in all candor that my feelings are mixed. I may look around, wondering who the whistlers are looking at, and will be surprised to meet their eyes.

Although I am pretty by traditional standards, my internalized feelings of having a not-acceptable body still operate. And I find my feminist consciousness, as a result, at odds with my old needs to be admired. We disabled women still haven't had our chance to be viewed as "sexy."

My disability did not affect my sexuality. The way in which I was treated and regarded, though, did affect my view of myself as a sexual being.

My mother was aware of our culture's virtual negation of disabled people's sexuality. She once told me that she had encountered this message in—of all places—a psychologist's office when she was told that her daughter would most likely become "a career girl" and shouldn't expect to marry. Mom countered this stereotype for me by openly sharing information about sex and my own body with me and by encouraging an attitude that I would be as "normal" as my girlfriends.

Because I had to be catheterized, however, I began to regard my genital area as not quite belonging to me; it belonged, instead, to the nurses, to the doctors, and to my Mom. I had little responsibility for it's functions. People who touched me there wore sterile gloves, or at least always washed their hands first. It never occurred to me to masturbate, or that I could experience pleasure from that part of me.

Years later, in therapy, I was encouraged to try masturbating. It was about that time that I recalled my earliest sexual memory, where at age 2, I had to have my urethra stretched so I could be catheterized. I recalled the doctor washing me with sudsy cotton balls, which felt good. I still don't remember what I'm sure must have followed: intense pain.

At age 12, when I was learning to catheterize myself, the nurse handed me a mirror so I could locate the opening of my urethra. I was startled to find the intricate shapes and contours that I had never thought to investigate.

Out to prove my femaleness, I was sexually active as a young adult. I've run across this pattern in many of the disabled women I've counseled (as well as in some able-bodied women). Now, though, I look back askance at the orgasms I faked, at the insecurity and fear, and at the desperate need to be liked and validated. I look back scornfully as well at the driving, constant pressure to be with-it and cool.

I'm still reclaiming my sexuality, now in a new and most special way: I would like to become pregnant. My husband and I have decided to spend this year preparing ourselves for this change and challenge by spending more time with children, talking to parents and clarifying our child rearing values. I have also taken time for visits to the genetic counselor (statistics reveal a slightly increased chance of my having a baby with a similar disability), and to the gynecologist, who is researching possible complications to my bladder function. I must clarify my own feelings: with the availability of amniocentesis and ultrasound, would I choose to abort a baby with a disability *like mine*? Could I risk further injury to my already limited bladder function with pregnancy?

These visits to doctors and these decisions about my body stir up many old and painful memories. But my husband is an unusually supportive man who is pleased to hold me when I need to cry. We laugh a lot together and tease each other and proudly plan our future together, a future that includes a baby. Perhaps our own. Perhaps adopted. Perhaps minority. Perhaps disabled.

I've always been fascinated by people's histories. I guess I'm my own prime subject in a life-long study of how people become who they are. These ponderings over my past and my identity are ongoing.

Many years ago, I became involved in a peer counseling network where I learned counseling skills and eventually became a trainer of other peer counselors. I learned an approach that taught me to explore and to express my own feelings and to assist others in doing the same. With my co-counselors, I learned to become sensitive to and challenging of one of the strongest sources of emotional distress in our culture: oppression.

Oppression is a heavy word, one that conjures up images of the Berlin Wall or the lynching rope. I use the term broadly to mean any behavior that mistakes a person for a stereotype or that *invalidates* someone on the basis of a particular characteristic that is different from the mainstream (for example, being too old or too young, being raised poor, displaying femaleness in a male role, having dark skin or a Jewish name). We are all, I believe, the target of a myriad of subtle oppressions that contribute to our chronic cultural malady of feeling not okay.

I was excited to grasp this concept. I could now combat oppression not just in peace marches and demonstrations, but in my personal relationships as well. I could challenge the expectations of others that imposed unnecessary limits on me—as a female, as a disabled person.

With my co-counselors, I focused singularly on the experience of being a woman and shared those occasions when I felt sometimes subtle, sometimes blatant restrictions imposed on my girl strengths. At the time I joined the supervision group at Boston Self Help Center, I had—amazingly enough—hardly even glanced at my being disabled as a possible source of such oppression. There were very few other disabled people in my co-counseling community to challenge my denial and as few able-bodied people aware enough to spot it.

The Boston Self Help Group was the catalyst that helped me bring my newly discovered "disabled" feelings to my co-counseling sessions where soon I was encouraged to involve my disabled friends. These two communities complimented each other nicely: the disabled community was eager to make use of my skills as a peer counselor trainer in the service of the Independent Living Movement and the co-counseling community was ready to challenge its own "able-bodiedism" by welcoming disabled people to its sessions.

I have learned about the necessity of having a peer, someone whose own personal knowledge of what I was sharing would reduce my fear of self-disclosure and allow me to really tell. For so long I had neither valued the associations I'd had with other disabled people nor even recognized my own disabledness. I remember so distinctly the relief I felt when I was able to discuss my bladder condition with another woman, she with a spinal cord injury; we each knew what it meant to have to catheterize ourselves.

And how delighted I came to feel upon finding others with skinny legs or awkward walks. I remember one disability workshop at which we held an evening stroll for people who walked funny. We imitated each other and laughed hilariously *with* each other.

What is a "peer"? In the context of counseling I have learned that a peer does not have to be someone with the same or even a very similar type of disability. What has seemed to be important for that special safety is instead that the peer be able to resonate with my experience. I remember, for example, being intrigued by a special connection I felt with a woman I met at a co-counseling session. She had a cleft lip. When we met, we discovered a common theme in our self-images: a sense of not having been *welcomed* into the world (due, we guessed, to the reactions of our parents and others at the time of our birth to the would-be-perfect babies).

The Something That Happened Before I Was Born

I have also learned about the importance of another role: the advocate, or *ally* as I like to term it. This is an able-bodied person who is familiar with and sensitive to the issues of disability and who, because of a *lack* of direct experience with the pain or stigma of disability, can offer a more objective, relaxed view—a different kind of safety. The ally's interest in disability may result from his or her own resonance with vulnerability. I'm not sure. But the role is a tricky one, easily confused with that of patron or helper. It's a role we must continue to train and support. It's a perspective from which I've received many valuable hours of insight.

There are few of us who have not experienced some kind of disability or significant illness in our lives. For that reason, the line separating the peer from the ally remains, in our civil rights struggle, a fuzzy one.

In my most vulnerable moments, in the confidence of a trusted peer or ally, I have allowed the yuckiest of feelings to emerge and present themselves to my consciousness: I am some monster from another place, disguised as a human. I must struggle to hide my true identity, for if I'm found out I will be killed.

I puzzle at these irrational subconscious thoughts. Where could these feelings have come from to a child of loving and devoted parents and so many well-meaning others? Is some part of me still trying to punish myself for the something-that-happened before I was born?

In graduate school and in the jobs I worked afterwards, the emphasis was very much geared toward helping disabled people *fit in, adjust to*, and *cope* with the world the way it is. As a result of my growing consciousness, I began to reevaluate this view. The world the way it is, in fact, is not a rational, welcoming place for people with disabilities (nor is it for anyone with "difference"). I realized I had to channel my energies into changing such a world, helping it to adapt, as well as to support the people who needed some help to function within it.

Soon after this realization (now 5 years ago), I quit my job at the hospital, wrote a grant proposal for a peer counseling program at Boston Self Help Center (which we were awarded), and became active in the disability rights movement. Now my favorite work activities involve training peer counselors and conducting disability awareness workshops in the community.

Social change, I believe, occurs at the level of the individual. It is so satisfying for me to see peer counselors not only gain skills as helpers, but also gain insight into themselves as disabled people. The development of peer counseling is, I believe, one of the most effective aspects of the Independent Living Movement. It not only increases the quality and quantity of much needed counseling resources, it also trains effective leaders in the movement. And when I conduct disability awareness workshops with school children, employers, health care workers, church groups, or whomever, my approach is that of training allies—able-bodied allies—to advocate for us (for themselves, for their family members, for their friends) in our struggle for civil rights, our liberation.

Impressions
Alan J. Brightman

Call Him Mr. Smith

To understand why this section isn't called "Conclusions," you have to meet a man I never met. I saw him only once, at a large special education conference several years ago. He spoke for 10 minutes, maybe 15. I've never forgotten him.

With the afternoon session about to begin, four men and one woman took their places on stage. The woman looked like a professional presenter, appropriately suited up, papers in hand, testing-testing the several microphones spaced along the table. The men looked like finalists from different bowling teams—sport shirts, smiles, and not an index card among them. The woman looked stern and anxious. The men looked friendly, unphased, and amused.

The room was filling noticeably.

"Good afternoon," the woman began, "my name is Dr. So-and-So. For the next hour and a half, we're going to be examining the experiences of recently de-institutionalized retarded adults living in the community." The men on stage continued to talk among themselves. "Seated here with me are four gentlemen, each of whom has spent more than 30 years of his life in a state school for the retarded. Today, each lives more or less independently right here in the Philadelphia area."

There were now roughly 250 people paying attention as the woman went on to refine the panel's task. "It's naturally assumed that moving from the institution to the community is the right way to go. I'm sure no one in this hall would argue with that." No one did. "But," she emphasized, "can we simply assume that once retarded people are placed in the community, the problem is solved? (Murmurs of dissent from some.) How carefully, in fact, have we examined the solution for the problems it may contain? That's what we've asked our panel of experts to help us do today: to help us understand what might *not be so terrific* about being a retarded person in the community."

Each of the panel members was asked to introduce himself and "to tell us about where you used to live and where you live now."

With his eyes locked on the microphone, the first panelist hurried through a quiet, measured response; he looked up only when he was done. And then his cheeks glowed pink as he erupted into a smile that seemed too wide for his face.

The filled room chuckled its encouragement, nodding almost too much.

The third speaker is the one I most remember; I'll call him Mr. Smith.[1]

---

[1] In the interest of accurate reporting, it needs to be noted that the woman introduced him only as "Artie"—just as she introduced and constantly referred to the other three only by their first names or nicknames. All were more than 50 years old. None was called Mister anything. Like perpetual children.

Impressions

Fifty-seven years old, Mr. Smith had spent all but the last 17 months of his life in two different state schools. He preferred not to dwell on those years, though, dismissing them categorically as "lost time." He wanted to talk instead about today, about "what bothers me most of all since I'm out."

"First," he began, "I don't like how they do roommates. You don't choose. They choose. You got no choice who you live with." Then, in a sly smiling aside he added, "You know who *they* are, don't you?" Mr. Smith had his finger on the pulse of the audience; most were *they's* themselves.

"Next," he went on, "I don't like it when I hear on the news about a house robbery and then they find out that the crook maybe was retarded so the judge lets him go free. Like the crook was too stupid to know what he was doing, I suppose?" He paused then added, "Bad for our image, in my opinion."

Mr. Smith was hot. The audience was his.

"Finally," he said, "I don't like all the trouble people have with coming up with a word to describe me. Like it makes them uncomfortable, in my opinion, to say I'm retarded. But then they don't know what other word to use instead. Seems to me I've heard them all."

The room chuckled again, this time more nervous than amused. Most, it felt, had been just where Mr. Smith was describing.

"So I'll tell you what," Mr. Smith continued. "I'm going to solve the problem today, once and for all, for everyone. It'll be easier for you and easier for me." Even the three male panel members were listening now. "From now on, the word you should use is . . . *retardate*."

The room didn't know how to react. Of all the suggestions he might have offered, why had he chosen the coldest, least personal, most clinical? Hushed whispering punctuated mostly silence. Mr. Smith wasn't finished.

"And from now on, the word I'll use to describe all of you is *normate*."

Several beats later, the room roared its approval, delighted at having been taken by Mr. Smith. No matter that he hadn't really solved the problem after all. He had at least acknowledged it.

We'd each, I was convinced, come up with our own solution.

I never got a chance to talk with Mr. Smith. When the presentation ended, he and his fellow presenters were hurriedly herded away. But I doubt I'll ever forget him, what he taught me, and how he made me feel.

Today, whenever I encounter someone struggling to find the "proper" disability term, I recall Mr. Smith's knowing smile . . . and try to hide my own. When I see outstretched hands sketch exaggerated quotation marks in the air to qualify use of the word "*normal*,"[2] Mr. Smith returns again, advising me to ignore.

Mr. Smith took an issue of importance to him, softened it with humor, and saw to it that none of its import would be lost on his intended audience. How different his approach was from the studied and all too grating castigations of the "spokes-persons" (disabled and non-disabled alike) who

---

[2] This particular histrionic is only slightly more common than the perplexing use of the disclaimer *whatever that means*, immediately following the word *normal*. In either case, with the word seemingly requiring such elaborate qualification, one wonders why another wasn't chosen in the first place.

seem ever poised to pounce on what they view as even the slightest semantic transgressions. The point here may be less one of substance than of style. Mr. Smith just happened to have both.

I remember him vividly and fondly. I wonder how many of my colleagues in the room do as well. Who else, I wonder, did he impress?

Which brings me to why I wanted you to hear about Mr. Smith in the first place.

In my earliest thinking about *Ordinary Moments*, I was certain that its final chapter would, well, conclude. Even before I enlisted the authors of the previous eight chapters, before I knew for sure which disabilities would be "represented" and which would not, I knew that I knew how it would end. I'd wrap it up, I figured, in thematic ribbons, making of this subject of disability a neat, ordered, and presentable package.

I'd talk about all those things we talk about when we talk about disability. Like how we don't talk about disability very much, like acceptance and rejection, joy and grief, expectations and disappointments. I hadn't read all those disability books for nothing; I was prepared to conclude even before I began.

And I was wrong. The package, I now realize, must remain untidy. For I, like you, have come to know a little about eight people during the course of *Ordinary Moments*. I didn't study them; I have no conclusions about them. I listened to them, spent some time with them. I have impressions, instead. I have subjective reactions. There's no truth or consequence in any of them.

There's no reason they should agree with or mean any more than your own.

Semantics

> *To grow up handicapped in America is to grow up in a society that, because of its misreading of the significance of disability, is never entirely human in the way it treats the person within.*
> Gliedman, J., and Roth, W., The Unexpected Minority:
> Handicapped Children in America, Harcourt Brace Jovanovich,
> New York, 1980 (p. 301)

How easy it is to romanticize the lives of people who are disabled, to make of them heroes or tragic victims, larger or smaller than life. How easy it is to think of them as quite unlike ourselves.

If I'm left with one impression that arches over all the others, it is that I and each of the people of *Ordinary Moments* are much more alike than not. Distancing strategies don't work for me; in my view, none of these people is heroic, none is tragic. Each is of rather common proportions.

But I'm troubled by this reaction; it sounds so glib, so safe, so much like the right thing to say. "Disabled people are just like you and me." "The disabled person, remember, is a person first; only then is he or she disabled." These platitudes are so easy and so empty. Adults escape into them often. Children see right through them. They're certainly not accurate. And they're certainly not what I mean.

I simply mean I'm impressed with how ordinary each is. How amusing, how dull, how tough, how weak, how reasonable, how heroic (at times), how tragic (at times). I'm impressed that none is a big deal, though each has been (and will, no doubt, continue to be) perceived as such by some.

I'm impressed by what each wrote, by how their words on paper sound so much like their words in everyday conversation. There could have been so much soapboxing here.

A disabled person. A person with a disability. Once I thought the difference was simply semantic.

Bag and Baggage and Politesse

The problem with disability is that it's just not polite. It lacks subtlety and decorum. It fights conformity. It whirrs or squeals or limps or twists or stumbles or . . .

It pays no attention to accepted social graces. It takes its own sweet time. It stands out in every crowd.

When will it ever learn just to fit in like the rest of us? When will it stop forcing us to notice it?

When will it finally learn some manners?

So that we—shrewd observers of the superficial—can be comfortable in its midst once and for all.

The Obstacle of Me

Often as I talked with the authors and read their words, I found myself asking questions that I'm certain many of us—even the most apparently accepting of us—have pondered: What kind of a disabled person would I make? Could I be as together as this one or that one? I doubted that I could.

I don't suffer minor setbacks gracefully. And disability seems to me not minor.

Was it pity I was feeling? I'm quick to answer no; it's not right to feel pity. (But was it?) Or was it admiration? Perhaps even envy?

Coming to know these individuals has made me begin to question me. That wasn't in the original plan, but it can't be avoided. More so since the book's been done, I wonder who and how I am. Who and how I affect.

Funny the handle you find on yourself when you spend much of your time with disabled people. I speak not only of the eight you've just come to know, but as well of the hundreds of others I've met and spent time with for a number of years. You develop a perspective on your concerns, what's important, what's trivial. That's different, I hope, from "There but for the grace of God go I."

But I don't know what to call it.

Maybe, then, among all those obstacles that need to be overcome, there's the obstacle of me. I'm a helper in the field, wondering who I am. Wondering, too, what I'm doing there, accomplishing there. Wondering who I'm helping there.

It's all a question of obstacles, isn't it? Removing the ones you can, overcoming the ones you can't. And being always on the lookout for the ones you didn't notice before. Physical ones. Interpersonal ones. Psychological ones.

The obstacle of me. There's nothing that the Architectural Barriers Board can do about that.

Impressions of Us

"Doesn't it make you sad to be with people like them?" It's a common question, one TAB[3] to another. Sometimes I'd be lying to answer no.

Mostly, though, I'm not made sad. I'm made angry, indignant, and embarrassed. For when I'm with "them," I become much more conscious of "us." And we don't look so good. Fact is, if you were to read the previous eight chapters again, attending this time not to "them" but to "us," I think you'll agree that we generally come across terribly. That impression should sadden all of us.

Recall, for example, those instances where so-called service providers rear their well-intentioned heads. For the most part, their words and their actions led to hurt. They served little and provided even less. Why is that? "Don't talk to disabled people about doctors?" Why is that?

And then there are the various images of us on the street, in the stairway or along the hall. Staring. Pointing. Making dumb, insensitive remarks. Unsubtle us. Unappealing us. We are a big part of my impressions.

Why should a book about "them" leave such a strong and unpleasant aftertaste of "us"?

A Closing Thought

If there is one common theme in each of the previous accounts, it is, in my view, that which is expressed in comments like: "I didn't want to be treated differently." I respect that. I think I understand what it means. And it confuses me.

Special treatment—be it the walking-on-eggs of some, the rejection (or non-acceptance) of others, or the cautious, stilted, or patronizing manner of still others—may be a necessary consequence of being disabled in a world discomforted by too much difference. We are unused to you. You

---
[3] TAB is an increasingly common reference to *temporarily able-bodied* individuals (six out of every seven individuals with a disability were not born disabled).

short circuit our spontaneity, you wrinkle the fabric of friendliness that each of us wears so stylishly in the company of our non-disabled peers. Too self-conscious, we are socially disheveled. We have to treat you differently, as something special.

At least at first.

So be patient with us. Be angry, too, if you will, but give us some time to get comfortable with ourselves. And, give us a hand when we stumble.

We need you to help us see you. So that soon we can hardly notice you at all.

Appendix

Some Personal Favorites

Like everything else about *Ordinary Moments*, the selection of books that follows is more subjective than definitive. With four exceptions, each book includes first-hand accounts of the disabled experience—living it or living with someone who's living it. With no exception (in my opinion), the books are also distinguished by being well written, in some instances thrillingly so.

The list could easily have been longer, but then, I worried, it might have hindered more than it helped. Some of your personal favorites, I'm sure, will be missing.

In its earliest draft, this list included brief editorial comments about each work. In the end, though, every comment sounded the same (more or less like: "This one's *really* terrific. Read it tomorrow and then tell all your friends about it."). So in lieu of cheerleading, I opted to accompany each book with one or more brief excerpts. I'm hopeful that any injustice to the authors is warranted by the gains in appreciation that these short samplings are designed to promote.

Blatt, B., **Exodus From Pandemonium: Human Abuse and a Reformation of Public Policy,** *Allyn & Bacon, Boston, 1970 (268 pp/hc)*

"In the institution, everyone waits—patients, attendants, doctors, the superintendent. But the patient's wait is longest: first, because it *is* longest and, second, because it usually is for no reason, toward no goal, no achievement. He waits for nothing. This is his destiny. And, if he is lucky, he is not surprised by its discovery." (p. 149)

"There doesn't appear to be a right way or a wrong way to interact with another human being, other than to know that the wrong way always involves thoughtlessness, a mechanistic approach—or ennui—that is determined irrespective of that human being, what he wants, or what he is." (p. 174)

Bogdan, R. (ed.), **Being Different: The Autobiography of Jane Fry.** *John Wiley & Sons, New York, 1974 (235 pp/hc)*

"This narrative, dealing with one person's life as she tells it, is presented as more than just a story. It may be engaging, personal, moving and enjoyable, as stories are, but its aim is one common in the social sciences: a better understanding of society, its institutions, and those who pass through them." (p. 1)

"Society is funny—first people put you in a position to make you withdraw, and then people get angry because you are withdrawing. That getting angry with you builds a higher wall between you and the society. The person who is pushed out has a tough time seeing what is happening. That's what was happening to me at this point." (p. 41)

Brightman, A., and Storey, K., **Ginny.** Scholastic Book Services, New York, 1978 (31 pp/pb)

"My friends and I have such a good time doing things that we forget about each other's sizes and shapes and freckles and fatness and skinniness and all those things that are different about each other. A difference doesn't matter so much when you're with friends." (p. 15)

Brightman, A., and Storey, K., **Hollis.** Scholastic Book Services, New York, 1978, (31 pp/pb)

"Sometimes the questions people ask are really upsetting. Like they'll ask, "How come you can't walk?". . . and I'm already walking. Or they'll say, "You walk like Donald Duck," or something like that." (p. 20)

Brown, H., **Yesterday's Child,** M. Evans and Co., New York, 1976 (209 pp/hc)

"A person's relationship with a handicapped child is a relationship quite unlike any other. Husbands and wives drift apart and marriages end; healthy children grow from dependence to adulthood and independence and eventually leave their parents; parents themselves grow old and die. But a handicapped child is with you from birth—forever. He or she is a responsibility that always hovers at the edge of your life." (p. 36)

"Moments of true peace come rarely in the lives of parents of handicapped children." (p. 67)

"My luck and my tragedy was Karen. She had begun as the pretty baby of my dreams and had turned my life into a nightmare—because of what she was and because of the person I was . . . I derived pleasure from being with Karen, when I wasn't wrestling with the problems she created just by living." (pp. 145–146)

Carrillo, A.C., Corbett, K., and Lewis, V., **No More Stares,** The Disability Rights Education and Defense Fund, Inc., Berkeley, CA, 1982 (128 pp/pb)

"There I am in the mirror. How do I look? Not so good. I can look in the mirror and I look great. Five minutes later I look again and I look awful. I see something wrong—a 'blemish.' I don't even need a mirror, I can feel this pimple. Why do I have to be disabled *and* have pimples?" (p. 25)

"Even with lots of great people on your side, *things* can really get you down." (p. 65)

Crews, H., **A Childhood: The Biography of a Place,** *G. K. Hall & Co., Boston, 1979*

"Right there, as a child, I got to the bottom of what it means to be lost, what it means to be rejected by everybody (if they had not rejected me, why was I smothered in shame every time they looked at me?) and everything you ever thought would save you. And there were long days when I wondered why I did not die, how I could go on mindlessly living like a mule or a cow when God had obviously forsaken me. But if I was never able to accept my affliction, I was able to bear it and finally to accept the good-natured brutality and savagery in the eyes of those who came to wish me well. Mainly because of Auntie's sheer wisdom and terror. She made me see that in this world there was much more to worry about than merely being crippled." (pp. 171–172)

Elliott, D.W., **Listen to the Silence,** *New American Library, New York, 1969 (224 pp/pb)*

"I think to myself, will I ever be like them, will I ever get out of here. If they keep me long enough I probably will be like them some day and I never will get out. I can't imagine myself being old and hairy and dirty and not caring, but maybe they also thought the same way at one time." (p. 9)

"In the morning the keys walk down the hall saying hello to every door. When they come to mine I wait holding the piece of bedspring but nothing happens. I hear Skinny swearing before he walks on to unlock all the others. Oh no, I think to myself. He's going to leave me locked in today and maybe from now on." (p. 86)

"Even the bad things were good when they ended." (p. 185)

Featherstone, H., **A Difference in the Family: Life With a Disabled Child,** *Basic Books, New York, 1980 (250 pp/hc)*

"This book is about . . . us, and people like us, more than it is about Jody, because Jody remains partly a mystery. He cannot talk. He cannot see. He cannot move about and explore the world. He cannot even play with toys, although he can smile and laugh and enjoys treats. It makes me sad to write this, but it is almost impossible for us to imagine his world. Perhaps for that reason I am more aware of the ways Jody has reshaped our understanding than of the ways we have shaped his." (p. 6)

"Most people have to face a reality before they can begin to weave it into their lives. But a realistic assessment of a child's limitations may take a long time, since children are complicated and sensible experts are sometimes hard to find." (p. 216)

Goffman, E., **Stigma: Notes on the Management of Spoiled Identity,** *Prentice-Hall, Engelwood Cliffs, NJ, 1963, (147 pp/pb)*

"I am suggesting, then, that the stigmatized individual—at least the 'visibly' stigmatized one—will have special reasons for feeling that mixed social situations make for anxious unanchored interaction. But if this is so, then it is to be suspected that we normals will find these situations shaky too." (p. 18)

"Apparently in middle class circles today, the more there is about the individual that deviates in an undesirable direction from what might have been expected to be true of him, the more he is obliged to volunteer information about himself, even though the cost to him of candor may have increased proportionately." (p. 64)

Greenfeld, J., **A Child Called Noah,** *Holt, Rinehart & Winston, New York, 1970 (189 pp/hc)*

". . . Noah is a tyrant of moods. He is deep, too: inscrutable—there is no other word for him. He is quick to copy, quick to react, but impossible when it comes to figuring out just what he's thinking." (p. 36)

"I really can't quite yet accept myself as the father of a Noah. I just can't cast myself in that part—which is, of course, my role for life." (p. 146)

"I'm not sure now we can ever get Noah to talk. I'm not sure any effort on our part is worthwhile. The sonofabitch demands so much—and gives back so little." (p. 152)

"Of course it is easy to sentimentalize: how having a Noah gives meaning and definition to one's life. How people without Noahs are constantly searching for humanistic dedications. How a Noah teaches one the values of the old verities. Bullshit! Without Noah we'd be freer to explore the boundaries of our own lives instead of constantly trying to pierce his perimeters." (p. 169)

Greenfeld, J., **A Place for Noah,** *Holt, Rinehart & Winston, New York, 1978 (310 pp/hc)*

"Noah pervades my life. Still I try not to think about him all the time. This morning I saw someone from the Knights of Columbus drive for retarded children. And I walked right by. I just did not want to think about the problem at that moment. I even resented being reminded of it. I hope someone is there tomorrow." (p. 94)

"I overheard a parent at Noah's school discussing the movie *The Exorcist*: 'That kid didn't seem so bad off to me,' she said. 'I wish my kid could say those words. I wish my kid could say anything.'" (p. 163)

"A child should not have to leave home just because his continued presence makes his parents unhappy." (p. 206)

Greig, D., and Brightman, A., **Laurie,** *Scholastic Book Services, New York, 1978 (31 pp/pb)*

"Sometimes, in a way, I feel like I'm missing out on things, and I really wish that I could see again. Like when I meet someone new and then someone else tells me that the person has green eyes or blond hair or something like that, I start wishing that I could see those things for myself. That's what I feel I miss most." (p. 17)

Heller, J., **Something Happened,** Alfred A. Knopf, New York, 1974 (569 pp/hc)

". . . or we will have to send Derek away early to a home for retarded people and never look at him again. We will erase him, cross him out, file him away—even though we go to visit him three or four times the first year, one or two times the second, and after that perhaps not at all, we will never really look at him again. We will put him out of sight, think of him less and less. He will visit *us*, maybe, in dreams."

"'I wonder how he's doing,' one of us might think of speculating from time to time, if either of us dared to face the consequences of a reply."

And later:

"'Whatever happened to him? You know, that kid we used to have? Derek, I think his name was. The one with something wrong. Are we still in touch with him?'" (p. 130)

Hunt, N., **The World of Nigel Hunt: The Diary of a Mongoloid Youth,** Garrett Publications, New York, 1967 (126 pp/hc)

"Do you remember earlier in this book I mentioned about my mother's illness and now with deep regret I have to tell you that she is *dead*, her breathing stopped on Thursday night, but I have been glad, because she is here at my house now. She knows I am being a nice brave boy, and I am not too sad. And now I am practically finished [writing] about [my school], and heard the fate of my poor mother. But she will be glad I am writing this book." (p. 113)

Jones, R., **The Acorn People,** Bantam Books, New York, 1977 (80 pp/pb)

"Martin was the most able-bodied child in our group. Like other blind children in camp, he had a constant smile and seemed in perpetual motion. Sitting still, he would rock forward and back. Even standing, he swayed rhythmically. I wondered what sound or unseen tide pulled at him." (p. 12)

"You might say she was captured by good intentions. Kids would huddle around her proposing things to do. It was as if she possessed some kind of magic. Well, maybe she did. After all, she stripped those labels off all of us. She gave us back the chance to be children. To dream and play." (p. 54)

Keller, H., **The Story of My Life,** Dell Publishing, New York, 1978, (416 pp/pb)

"Very few of the books required in the various courses are printed for the blind, and I am obliged to have them spelled into my hand. Consequently I need more time to prepare my lessons than other girls. The manual part takes longer, and I have perplexities which they have not. There are days when the close attention I must give to details chafes my spirit, and the thought that I must spend hours reading a few chapters, while in the world without other girls are laughing and singing and dancing, makes me rebellious; but I soon recover my buoyancy and laugh the discontent out of my heart." (p. 90)

"The hands of those I meet are dumbly eloquent to me. The touch of some hands is an impertinence. I have met people so empty of joy, that when I clasped their frosty finger tips it seemed as if I were shaking hands with a northeast storm. Others there are whose hands have sunbeams in them, so that their grasp warms my heart." (p. 116)

Konrad, G., **The Case Worker,** Bantam Books, New York, 1976 (182 pp/pb)

"Since my job is to protect children and safeguard the interests of the state, the most I can do is reconcile him with his circumstances and oppose his propensity for suffering. I do what the law and my fumbling judgement permit; then I look on, mesmerized, as the system crushes him." (p. 15)

"For years now I have been bustling from door to door and courtroom to courtroom with a briefcase full of modest but futile petitions and of intelligent but unintelligible decisions. Overburdened by [my clients'] frustrations, the sympathy in me has become as gritty as a handful of burning sand." (p. 93)

"Actually, what I do amounts to nothing. I regulate the traffic of suffering, sending it this way and that, passing on the loads that pile up on me to institutions or private citizens. But for the most part I wait, and try to stop others from doing anything." (p. 109)

Kovic, R., **Born on the Fourth of July,** Pocket Books, New York, 1977 (224 pp/pb)

"I feel like a big clumsy puppet with his strings cut. I learn to balance and twist in the chair so no one can tell how much of me does not feel or move anymore. I find it easy to hide from most of them what I am going through. All of us are like this. No one really wants too many people to know how much of him has really died in the war." (p. 37)

"I am alone again. I have been lying in Room 17 for almost a month. I am isolated here because I am a troublemaker. I had a fight with the head nurse on the ward. I asked for a bath. I asked for the vomit to be wiped up from the floor. I asked to be treated like a human being." (p. 128)

Lifchez, R., and Winslow, B., **Design for Independent Living: The Environment and Physically Disabled People,** University of California Press, Berkeley, 1979 (208 pp/pb)

"Major problems for many disabled people occur as a result of society's unwillingness to view them as sexual beings and potential mates.

Institutions traditionally treat them as children, separating the sexes and regarding expressions of affection as a perversion or inappropriate behavior that must be discouraged." (p. 70)

"In Berkeley we have confronted a sizable population of disabled people who know the joy of small, self-sufficient acts; who are very much in touch with their bodies; who often spend long periods of time alone and have come to know that aloneness is not necessarily loneliness; to whom being alive and well and active in the world is rarely taken for granted." (p. 149)

Massie, R., and Massie, S., **Journey,** *Warner Books, New York, 1976 (462 pp/pb)*

"At home we tried to treat his growing physical infirmities matter-of-factly . . . as something annoying. About one thing we were very strict. No self-pity. Even if his legs were being twisted, there was no reason that his soul should be. We kept insisting that he think of himself not as an invalid but as someone temporarily out of commission, *only temporarily.* Keep the attitude positive; tomorrow will be better. But outside, no one would let him forget for a moment that he was 'different' and 'ill.'" (p. 115)

"Early in our experience I realized that the world would accept us—and Bobby—only to the extent that we did not bother them too much. That is, if we pretended." (p. 193)

"His life is dominated from the outside. He is subject not only to the limitations of the disease but to a dependence on the kindness, generosity, and sheer physical presence of other people. To have to ask for everything, to have to involve others in even the smallest personal decision, to be always grateful, is a kind of torture from which most of us—without even thinking about it—are blessedly free." (p. 328)

McGrath, E.J., **An Exceptional View of Life: The Easter Seal Story,** *Island Heritage, Ltd., Hawaii, 1977 (64 pp/hc)*

"In this book, only the words on this page are written by adults. All other words and pictures in the book come from the minds and hearts of exceptional children." (p. 4)

"Things that make me sad is when something goes wrong, like in a family. Like when your parents are crying and you feel like you're in the middle. Sometimes I feel like I'm responsible, like I caused the trouble, and I don't know why. Mainly, when my stepfather and mother fight, that's when I feel like I'm in the middle. It doesn't have anything to do with cerebral palsy, though." (p. 35)

"Now I can dress myself. I have a bowel program. I can transfer myself to a bed and get up a hill on a wheelchair. I like to try things new myself. Opening a door is one of the things I'd like to try." (p. 43)

"Due to difficulties beyond our control this story will not be continued because the writer had to be taken to the funny farm." (p. 53)

Montagu, A., ***The Elephant Man: A Study in Human Dignity,*** Ballantine Books, New York, 1971 (153 pp/pb)

"There stood revealed the most disgusting specimen of humanity that I have ever seen." (p. 16)

"Merrick, I may say, was now one of the most contented creatures I have chanced to meet. More than once he said to me: 'I am happy every hour of the day'... One thing that always struck me as sad about Merrick was the fact that he could not smile. Whatever his delight might be, his face remained expressionless. He could weep but he could not smile." (pp. 32–33)

Pieper, E., ***Sticks and Stones: The Story of Loving a Child,*** Human Policy Press, Syracuse, NY, undated (88 pp/pb)

"It was painful to see all the other mothers holding and cuddling, tenderly examining and feeding their babies, and never to have held mine. It was awful to walk through the halls like a homeless waif, fearing to intrude on someone's joy in the course of making small talk. I felt terrible to know that my baby was not in the nursery, to know that while the other husbands and grandparents clucked proudly through the nursery window, our baby lay alone and forsaken, probably in a haze of pain." (p. 10)

"What is unique to the medical world is that here, where one's very life and destiny are at stake, one has less recourse to social justice than in any other sphere." (p. 15)

"Jeff is neither my burden nor my chastisement, although his care requires more than I want to give at times. He is not an angel sent for my personal growth or my future glory; he is not a punishment for my past sins. He is a son." (p. 88)

Potok, A., ***Ordinary Daylight,*** Bantam Books, New York, 1980 (243 pp/pb)

"I was now blind, blind like them. Blind meant lonely and abandoned, cared for by special people, sanguine, dour, also lonely. Blind meant shuffling, groping, forlorn. It meant cheap paper crookedly stapled, badly mimeographed. How long could I postpone meeting others like me? I wanted to sleep through that Christmas." (pp. 3–4)

"In a strange sense, I had also felt relief. I was no longer responsible. I didn't have to struggle. I didn't have to be excellent or successful. Even the grimmest Soviet doctor supervising production workers in a tractor factory would have excused me from labor. I had a note from home, valid for life, permitting me to do nothing." (p. 86)

"I once thought that I was the most exotically maimed and deprived person imaginable. But with astonishing rapidity, others have caught up and surpassed me. Mine is no longer the most unique, complex, or insurmountable problem the world has ever known. Once I wouldn't have agreed to share the rotten-luck award with left-brained musicians or right-brained lawyers, not with flaccid movie heroes or bedridden athletes. But in my unexpected life, I'm no longer alone." (pp. 238–239)

Sheed, W., **People Will Always Be Kind,** *Farrar, Straus & Giroux, New York, 1973 (384 pp/hc)*

"The braces arrived, gaunt steel scaffoldings smothered in straps, and he was jimmied into them and strapped tight and hoisted aloft, like a knight helpless in his armor. It was a giddy feeling, lurching about at this altitude, with his feet trailing off in the distance. He jerked a leg in a memory of walking, and only Mrs. Schmidt, a former circus strong man, it turned out, kept him from crashing to the floor. His knees hurled themselves against the leather caps, they would certainly flop out in a moment. He was scared spitless that he would just fall apart if he tried to move again. Straw would fly out of his chest. But Mrs. Schmidt was everywhere, under his armpits, around his chest, doing it all." (p. 46)

"He took the number 5 bus home, and nobody offered him a seat. And for the first time, until now, he felt like shouting, 'Offer me a seat, you bastards. You've got everything else.'" (p. 168)

Shelley, M., **Frankenstein: Or, The Modern Prometheus,** *Dell Publishing, New York, 1975 (221 pp/pb)*

"I am thy creature, and I will be even mild and docile to my natural lord and king, if thou wilt also perform thy part, that which thou owest me. Oh. Frankenstein, be not equitable to every other, and trample upon me alone, to whom thy justice, and even thy clemency and affection, is most due . . .

"Believe me, Frankenstein: I was benevolent; my soul glowed with love and humanity: but am I not alone, miserably alone? You, my creator, abhor me; what hope can I gather from your fellow-creatures, who owe me nothing?" (p. 100)

Sullivan, M.B., Brightman, A.J., and Blatt, J. **Feeling Free,** *Addison-Wesley Publishing Co., Reading, PA, 1979 (192 pp/pb)*

"I used to feel that I couldn't ask anybody for help, that I should do everything on my own. That's because I thought it would be better to try and hide my problem." (p. 52)

"Joey, sometimes I HATE you! It's not fair. Why do I always have to stay in and play with you? Man, Mike just got a new glove, and he said I could try it out this afternoon when he's up at bat. But no, I can't go! I bet I'm the only kid in the whole world who has to stay in and play with his older brother. Well, I don't *want* to play with you, and I don't have to and no one can make me. Do you want to play catch?" (p. 56)

Trumbo, D., **Johnny Got His Gun,** Bantam Books, New York, 1976 (243 pp/pb)

"He had no legs and no arms and no eyes and no ears and no nose and no mouth and no tongue. What a hell of a dream. It must be a dream." (p. 62)

"He couldn't live like this because he would go crazy. But he couldn't die because he couldn't kill himself." (p. 63)

"And to him who had harmed nobody they were saying goodnight goodbye stay where you are don't give us any trouble you are beyond life you are beyond death you are even beyond hope you are gone you are finished forever goodnight and goodbye." (p. 236)

Wright, D., **Deafness: A Personal Account,** Penguin Press, London, 1969 (182 pp/pb)

"So far as cripples are concerned, pity is no virtue. It is a sentiment that deceives its bestower and disparages its recipient.

Zola, I., **Missing Pieces: A Chronicle of Living With a Disability,** Temple University Press, Philadelphia, 1982 (246 pp/hc)

"There on the other side of the room was Mr. Veere. It was a case of 'like at first sight.' He was a stockily built man, early thirties, in a red turtleneck sweater. His large mustache surrounded a full, friendly smile. A glance told me he had little physical mobility. His face, by contrast, was exceedingly alive. His lips, eyes, even nose seemed to take on the liveliness absent in the rest of his body." (p. 96)

"I simply could not find the right timing for offering him another puff or another sip. He could ask, of course, but obviously this was a bit of a drag. I knew he was aware of this. He may not have felt awkward, but I did. He was giving me a peek into the two-sided nature of social interaction with someone severely handicapped, and it was driving me up the wall." (p. 130)